The Last Twelve Years

1948–1959

The Royal Berkshire Regiment
(49th and 66th)

The Last Twelve Years
1948–1959

Major F. Myatt MC

Published by
The Trustees
The Wardrobe Museum Trust
58 The Close
Salisbury
Wiltshire SP1 2EX

ISBN 0–9540365–0–6
First published 2001

Designed by students at the
Department of Typography & Graphic Communication
The University of Reading

Printed by the
Department of Typography & Graphic Communication
The University of Reading

Author: Major F. Myatt MC
The proceeds of this publication are to be donated to the
Wardrobe Museum Trust.

Foreword

Brigadier D.W.B.T. Hogg's original Foreword to *The Last Twelve Years* (p. vi) sets the scene for this new printing.

This Foreword, which I have been privileged to write, continues his theme in emphasising the active part played by the Royal Berkshire Regiment in its many peacekeeping rôles as the British Empire handed over power in its old colonial territories. Vivid descriptions of the numerous actions and incidents around the world flow through the story interspersed with training, ceremonial and sporting events which give form to the balance of life in an Infantry Regiment.

Major Freddie Myatt's original account of the last twelve years in the life of the Royal Berkshire Regiment follows those of F.L. Petre and Gordon Blight (1920–47). His account covers the years of postwar political and internal financial reform which saw the British Army and particularly the Infantry, steadily reduced in numbers.

In 1949 the 2nd Battalion amalgamated with the 1st Battalion becoming the last remaining Regular unit. In turn, the 1st Battalion was amalgamated with the Wiltshire Regiment in 1959 to form the Duke of Edinburgh's Royal Regiment. It will be noted that the Territorial Army 4/6th Battalion remained intact until 1967 when it became part of the new Wessex Volunteers (TAVR).

The reduction in Regular Infantry continued in 1994 when the Duke of Edinburgh's Royal Regiment amalgamated with the Gloucestershire Regiment to form the Royal Gloucestershire, Berkshire and Wiltshire Regiment in today's Regular army.

The scale of change dictated by a changing, more technological world, created and continues to create, major challenges in meeting future defence needs. The successful adjustment to those challenges is the hallmark of the high standing and effectiveness of our Regiments of the Line.

In the last twelve years of the Royal Berkshire Regiment these ever changing events and challenges were met and overcome by a full life of operations, training, sport and ceremonial – the inspiration of all Infantrymen in peace and war as described in these pages.

The long history of the Regiment with its symbolic China Dragon cap badge and its regimental traditions handed down through the centuries covers a magnificent record of service. Maiwand, Tofrek, Bourlon Wood, Kohima, to name some milestones in its life, were outstanding examples of courage and endurance but behind all these trials and successes in the life of the Regiment lies the words 'Regimental Spirit'.

The Spirit of a Regiment through its historic past, raises morale to the highest levels, without which no Infantry Regiment can succeed when times are hard and life is rough and tough.

The Last Twelve Years exemplified this spirit carried on today in its Regimental Successors – The Royal Gloucestershire, Berkshire and Wiltshire Regiment.

L.J.L. Hill

January 2001

Foreword to the first printing

The euphoria of the period immediately following the end of the Second World War soon gave place to the bleak realisation that the world would never be the same place again. The great victories of the previous years were already fading. In their place we saw an overstretched British Army, consisting for the great part of young National Service men, well led by a cadre of experienced Regular Officers, Warrant Officers and Sergeants. They strove desperately, and on the whole successfully, to control a situation where country after country rose in an almost universal desire to achieve independence from their erstwhile Colonial rulers. The task mainly fell on the shoulders of the Infantry. This is a story which may be taken as typical of the role played by a Line regiment of the time.

It was inevitably rather a depressing period for the British Army. This account has deliberately been written for the most part in the sort of low key which perhaps best reflects the atmosphere of the times, although it is fortunately not without a leavening of humour too.

I am proud to have been associated with soldiers of the calibre of those whose service is chronicled in these pages. They were young and relatively inexperienced, in the main, but they worthily upheld the great traditions of the Regiment.

Brigadier D.W.B.T. Hogg CBE
Colonel of the Royal Berkshire Regiment
1956–59

Acknowledgements

The Last Twelve Years was first published and printed in 1988. Unfortunately, copy went to the printer before all the typescript errors had been corrected. The decision was made that the book should not go on sale. The subsequent death of the author, Major Freddie Myatt, resulted in a lengthy lapse in the production of this corrected version.

Students and staff at the Department of Typography & Graphic Communication of The University of Reading had, over a number of years, designed, typeset and published four books for the Royal Berkshire Regiment 'Kitchener Battalions' project. In 1999 the Department was asked if students would take on *The Last Twelve Years*. This was agreed. Sam Dallyn and Neil Stevens, under the tutorship of Martin Andrews, took on the book as a third-year project for the 1999/2000 academic year.

The original text had already been scanned at the Wardrobe and errors corrected. The opportunity was taken to add a name and place index and to incorporate more photographs. Special thanks go to John Peters, my predecessor as Curator, for locating the original photographs, producing and captioning the additional ones and extensively proof reading the draft prior to submission to the students.

The project was not completed within the academic year. However, under Mick Stocks and Paul Luna, the staff of the department took on the commitment to complete the design and publication process. Without their involvement it is highly unlikely that this book would ever be published.

Thanks too go to Mrs Elizabeth Diacon, Freddie Myatt's widow, for generously agreeing to the copyright of the book being passed to the Trustees of the Wardrobe and Museum Trust.

Finally, I am grateful to John Hill for his advice and for agreeing to provide a Foreword to this edition.

David Chilton
Curator
The Salisbury Museum of the
Royal Gloucestershire, Berkshire and
Wiltshire Regiment
Salisbury
January 2001

Contents

Illustrations

1 Eritrea

On 4 January 1948 the 2nd Battalion The Royal Berkshire Regiment, with few regrets, left Rangoon on *HT Scythia*, under the command of Lieutenant Colonel W.A. Bickford, en route for an unknown destination. Burma was the country in which the Battalion had played a distinguished part in the defeat of the Japanese less than three years before and in which they had been in garrison since. As the Battalion left, the country was in the throes of independence, with all the unlovely symptoms which have become a familiar scene in almost every country in the same position since. Armed gangs of young, Japanese-trained hooligans roamed the streets, paying off old scores. Murders were of such common occurrence prompting the author of the *China Dragon* notes for May 1947 to comment that in Rangoon local marksmen spent the hours of darkness carrying out their own version of star classification tests, then the method of assessing skill at arms in the Army. He added the sardonic comment 'We understand that one policeman equals one star, an arrangement infinitely superior to our own'. This atmosphere, heightened as it was by unrepaired roads, the rapid encroachment of the jungle, and a general sense of decay, made their feelings understandable. In spite of it all the Battalion was destined to stay to the bitter end, being the last British battalion to go.

Although British troopships were never famed for the comfort of their troop decks, the Battalion made the best of it. After an uneventful voyage they disembarked on 17 January at Port Said, and went to a transit camp at Tel-el-Kebir. Here they spent two nights in such unrelieved squalor that many members began to feel that they might have done better to have stayed in Burma after all. But then, as often happens, things changed for the better. On 20 January they moved to Moascar, a pleasant camp on the Suez Canal, where the Battalion had coincidentally been stationed in 1937, and immediately found themselves among friends.

In 1948 the Egyptians were not overtly anti-British and, with obvious differences due to the war, the Battalion settled down to a peace-time routine which was not in essence very different from the one which it had followed eleven years before. The chief trouble was one inseparable from post-war soldiering, a chronic shortage of man-power, which soon resulted in the placing of B Company in suspended animation on 16 February. This, combined with the detachment of A and Support Companies to Kassassin, left very few men available. Nevertheless the Battalion set a high standard in all things so that even an ex-member of the Afrika Corps was heard to comment approvingly that at last a 'proper' Regiment had arrived in the station.

Here the Colours were unpacked for the first time since before the war, and were found to be somewhat frail (which since they had been carried since 1882 is not surprising) but otherwise in better condition than might have been expected after years in store. They were carried on Church Parade on Sunday

21 March as part of the Tofrek celebrations, which also included the Beating Retreat by the Band and Drums in full dress, a spectacle not seen since the far-off days of 1939. Less formal aspects of the celebrations included a fun fair with donkey and camel rides, and an all-ranks dance. This pleasant interlude was to be of short duration, however, for on 11 April the Commanding Officer was told that the Battalion was on 24 hours notice to fly to Eritrea where trouble was expected. On 12 April Tactical Headquarters, A Company, and one platoon of C Company went to Kabrit. The next day they flew to Asmara, the capital of Eritrea, followed over the next few days by the remainder of the Battalion, some by air and the rest by sea. The Armoured Car Platoon went by road via Khartoum, and with the arrival of the rear party by sea on 30 April the Battalion was complete in its new location, the first time it had been fully concentrated for two years.

Eritrea had been an Italian colony, but in 1948 was being administered by Great Britain pending a final decision on its future. It was a mainly mountainous country, bounded on the east by the Red Sea and on the south by Ethiopia. It had a mixed population of Coptic Christians and Moslems, together with a considerable number of the original Italian colonists, who were tolerated but by no means liked. The present trouble arose from the fact that, although Italy had renounced her African Empire, she retained her claim to some sort of trusteeship. This was a most unlikely prospect and one regarded with horror by the inhabitants who, whatever their differences, were united in their detestation of their erstwhile rulers. The immediate cause of apprehension on the part of the authorities was the forthcoming elections in Italy out of which claims for an interest in the future of Eritrea might be made.

Rather to their surprise, and perhaps with mild disappointment, the Battalion arrived to find that neither emergency nor undue tension appeared to exist. They found themselves in the capital Asmara, a modern, pleasant town which, at a height of 7,500 feet above sea-level was blessed with an ideal climate. No proper barrack accommodation was available, but a week or so after its arrival the Battalion took over the airport buildings. They were modern and potentially well suited as accommodation, but were initially in a somewhat rundown state, particularly as regards the plumbing which was well up (or perhaps down) to colonial Italian standards. Fortunately the local Public Works Department was both efficient and co-operative so that in a very short time the Battalion was comfortably settled in. Initially it was purely a peace-time routine. Khaki drill was worn by day and battledress by night, a comfortable arrangement made possible by the climate and, although there were plenty of flies, there were no mosquitoes.

The town, which the Battalion lost no time in visiting, offered a wide range of entertainment, too much indeed for some of the younger members of the Battalion until they learnt the hard way. In particular venereal disease was rife. That autumn for example, of thirty-nine suspected prostitutes picked up by the police, all but one was infected.

Stealing was also prevalent. Indeed so bad did it become that the

Commanding Officer offered a reward of five pounds, a considerable sum by 1948 standards, for information leading to conviction.

Empire Day was duly celebrated on 24 May, followed on 4 June by further rejoicing on the Silver Jubilee of King George VI and Queen Elizabeth. A number of Battalion families arrived in station at the same time. They were followed by further celebrations of the King's birthday on 10 June, so that for a period life seems to have consisted of an endless round of parties.

At the same time however tension was rising. The immediate cause of the trouble was the Shifta, armed bandits who robbed, and often killed, defenceless people, but melted away into the vast expanses of mountainous desert whenever they were opposed by real force. As is usually the case with elusive, lightly armed opponents, patrols from the Battalion worked hard and with comparatively little to show for their efforts. The mere fact of their presence to the locals was a boost to morale however, and occasionally there were more tangible successes when members of hostile bands were killed in brief firefights. In these operations the Battalion worked in close conjunction with the British-led Eritrea police and with their auxiliaries the Banda, groups of armed local tribesmen, many of whom were themselves ex-Shifta. Although not always completely reliable they were nevertheless useful allies because they had the ability to move as quickly and easily across difficult country as their opponents.

There were also political undertones, mainly due to fears that the hated Italians would somehow regain control. Matters were made worse by the Emperor of Abyssinia, Haile Selassie, who offered the local Unionist Party armed support in order to prevent such a contingency. As the Shifta tended to favour union with Ethiopia (as far as they favoured any sort of rule) the opportunities for trouble were obvious. Ironically enough Great Britain gave regular consignments of arms to the Emperor, and the task of escorting such convoys from the coast to the Ethiopian border fell to the Battalion. Once across the border it was feared that the consignments were frequently looted by the local warlords, who had scant regard for the Emperor's central government in Addis Ababa. An officer who served with the Battalion remembered with mixed amusement and irritation that the local Shifta always seemed to be particularly well supplied with ammunition soon after fresh supplies of arms had been received.

On 9 August all were cheered beyond measure by the departure of the Advance Party for the United Kingdom, but on 14 September it was announced that the Battalion was to remain in the Middle East after all. This had an inevitable detrimental effect on morale, but it soon recovered.

On 12 June A Company had departed to Nairobi on a secret mission which on 24 August was revealed as helping to escort a large number of Jews to Palestine, an adventurous and far-ranging trip. Fortunately the Jews realised that they were going to their promised land and remained co-operative throughout. The Company did not actually rejoin the Battalion until 1 October.

Political tension continued, due mainly to uncertainty. As the Four Power

Committee, consisting of representatives from Great Britain, the United States, France and the Soviet Union, the chances of agreement were slight since the Soviet Union opposed every decision on principle.

Shifta activity continued. The Battalion laid on an impressive fire-power demonstration, which included support weapons and the Armoured Car Platoon, and which impressed the local citizens. Next day, 10 September, the Colours were lodged in the Bank and the Mess silver sent to the Ordnance depot, presumably to allow the Battalion to undertake large scale mobile operations, the return of the Advance Party also being asked for. In view of the chronic manpower shortage in the British Army, all National Service soldiers were to be retained for an extra three months, a decision which appears to have been accepted philosophically by the single men but less so by the married ones.

Meanwhile a considerable amount of training was carried out, together with a sports meeting and a rifle meeting. The latter was in preparation for the Command Rifle Meeting in Khartoum in which the Battalion did well. Some light relief was afforded by a perimeter sentry who opened fire after challenging, only to find next morning that his victim had been an unfortunate donkey.

Attention was now largely focused on the forthcoming amalgamation parade in which the 2nd Battalion was to be metamorphosed into the 1st Battalion. The Colours were brought from the Bank and two expert needle-women amongst the families, Mrs Bromhead and Mrs Stroud, spent many hours repairing them for what was to be their last public appearance. The 1st Battalion cadre arrived on 24 November and practice began in earnest for the parade in March 1949. At this time D Company was re-formed as a cadre company. Fortunately the situation in the country remained quiet so that Christmas celebrations were not interrupted. Very early in the New Year 1949 the Battalion was informed that it would remain in Eritrea. This at least offered some continuity, and more families were allowed out. In January too there arrived supplies of the new officers' badges and buttons. The familiar bee-hive shaped coil of cord, representing rope to commemorate the Regiment's naval connections, was replaced by a flat, all-metal cap badge, again showing (in different form) the coil and dragon motif. Collar badges were China Dragons in gilt or bronze depending on the order of dress, while the buttons bore a silver dragon on a gilt background. These new

1. Lt Col Bickford leading the march past on the amalgamation of the 1st and 2nd Battalions, Asmara, 5 March 1949.

embellishments came in good time for the amalgamation parade, to which much of the Battalion's efforts were by then directed.

The actual day of the parade was on 5 March 1949 and, as was to be expected, the weather was fine. The ceremony took place at the airport before a large crowd of spectators, both Colours being trooped. The salute was taken by General Sir John Crocker GCB KCB DSO MC, GOC Middle East. The Kaid, GOC Sudan (under whose command the Battalion came) and Major General L.G. Whistler CB CSO were also present. A particularly warm welcome was extended to Brigadier D.W.B.T. Hogg MBE, who was then serving at GHQ Middle East, and who had commanded the 1st Battalion in Germany in 1946/7. Unfortunately, General Sir Miles Dempsey KCB CBE DSO MC Colonel of the Regiment, was unable to attend due to other military commitments. Numerous messages of loyalty and good wishes were sent and received, including one from HM King George VI to the Colonel of the Regiment.

The parade was followed by Luncheon in the Officers' Mess, by a ball given by the Warrant Officers and Sergeants that evening (which the Commander-in-Chief attended) and by an all ranks dance on the following Monday.

The parade, in spite of its significance to the Regiment, made virtually no difference to daily routine. Tofrek was celebrated as usual on 22 March, but the very next day four refrigerator vans carrying supplies were held up by armed Shifta, while the District Commander, following close behind in his car, was robbed of thirty shillings by the same gang. They tried to take his watch as well, but after vigorous protests on his part and an explanation as to who he was from his Italian driver (nervous no doubt, as he had every right to be, in such company) he was graciously allowed to keep it, which added a touch of musical comedy to the proceedings.

Other troubles continued to occur. A police raid on the headquarters of the youth section of the Unionist Party caused some rioting and resulted in the imposition of a curfew in Asmara. Meanwhile the Shifta had struck again, a

2. Loading mules in preparation for an anti-Shifta operation, Eritrea.

gang of seven raiding a cafe just outside the town and killing an Italian before decamping. Patrols from the Battalion went out but found nothing. For the first time they were wearing hats, jungle, which authority had decreed to be more suitable headgear for operations than the rather hideous khaki beret, shaped rather like a cowpat, which was then in general use.

On 20 May 1949 a company of the 1st Battalion The South Wales Borderers arrived from Khartoum to reinforce the Battalion, which was so much below strength that it was rapidly becoming impossible to carry out its duties. Four days later, on Empire Day, they marched through the town, with the band and drums, the carriers, and the armoured cars, as a show of force, a demonstration which cooled the ardour of potential rioters considerably.

Early in 1950 the remainder of The South Wales Borderers also moved to Eritrea, the country thereafter being divided between the two regiments. This did not of course prevent joint operations by both Battalions when occasion warranted them, and also made it possible for one or the other to carry out the occasional exercise.

The immediate threat of trouble still remained however, with the Shifta becoming bolder, so that the sensible precaution of convoying all vehicles had to be taken. Patrolling increased in intensity although time was still found to establish a range camp at Keren.

On 7 June some light relief was provided by the disappearance of a milestone on the Massawa road, and the local Director of the Public Works Department wrote a personal letter to the Commanding Officer voicing mild suspicions that members of the Battalion might be involved. As soon as it was ascertained that the stone bore the magic numbers '49' and '66' suspicion became certainty and steps were taken to recover it. Fortunately the PWD officers were on good terms with the Battalion and when the

3. A Support Company Staghound armoured car ditched near the Abyssinian border.

significance of the numbers was explained to them they good-naturedly agreed to replace the stone and say no more about it.

Soon after this incident there occurred a change of Commanding Officers when, on 6 July, Lieutenant Colonel H. Du Pré Finch DSO took over from Lieutenant Colonel Bickford, having handed over to him in Burma three years earlier. They had both had distinguished wartime careers in Burma where Lieutenant Colonel Bickford had commanded the 1st Battalion and Lieutenant Colonel Finch the 2nd Battalion. Soon after this his friends in the Battalion were delighted to hear that Captain A.F.E. Lucas of the Regiment had been awarded the Distinguished Service Order for gallantry in Malaya.

On 4 September a platoon of The South Wales Borderers got lost in difficult, broken, country but were found by search parties thirty miles off their intended course.

On 11 October 1949 the United Nations Sub-Committee decided that Eritrea should be partitioned, the Western Province should go to the Sudan and the remainder to Ethiopia. However, within a fortnight and before any-one could complain (for it is needless to say that few people approved the decision) the old military adage, order, counter-order, disorder was again proved true by the announcement that the decision had been reversed pend-ing the results of a fact-finding commission.

On 22 October the Battalion suffered its first operational casualties when Privates Haines and McDermott were killed when the vehicle in which they were travelling on a Shifta patrol skidded over a steep drop. A few days later a patrol of The South Wales Borderers retaliated while escorting an Italian vehicle by killing one Shifta and wounding a second.

Things remained fairly quiet thereafter until the New Year, but on 21 January the native quarter of Asmara was the scene of vicious rioting. The trouble started when Moslems threw a bomb at a Coptic funeral procession, and the situation quickly became serious. D Company, the only one imme-diately available, did what it could, but as it was far too thin on the ground to be effective, rioting continued unabated. The next day three more com-panies and the armoured cars were sent in. Even that force was barely sufficient to control the situation which, on 24 February, resulted in the burn-ing down of the native market. Finally, on the next day the combined appeals of the religious leaders of both factions, heavy rain and, it must be pre-sumed, sheer exhaustion, finally brought an uneasy calm to the town. Asmara remained out of bounds to the troops for some time, peace being maintained by regular patrolling. One feature of these affairs was the use of arson to discourage the other side. On one occasion an officer in an armoured car saw a native in the act of setting fire to a building and, still in the armoured car, ordered the driver to take his vehicle inside. This he did, both to the astonishment of the would-be arsonist and, it is to be feared, to the considerable detriment of the building concerned. Precautions were sub-sequently taken to establish observation posts on commanding features which, in conjunction with large quantities of dannert wire to block approaches, did much to help matters. The situation was made worse by having to maintain a company detachment, relieved fortnightly, in Adi Ugri about 30 miles away. Although necessary, the task made considerable inroads into the rather scanty manpower available.

Operations in the countryside were much helped at this time by the use of a flight of Spitfires. These were subsequently replaced by Beaufighters and finally, in July 1950 by a Royal Artillery OP flight. Both crews and ground staff lived in the Battalion's messes with their opposite numbers in the Battalion, which made for a close and fruitful liaison. Social life was further varied by visits by members of the Royal Navy whose ships visited Massawa from time to time.

At this time all ranks were saddened by news of the death of Major General R.J. Collins CB CMG DSO who had been Colonel of the Regiment during the difficult days of the Second World War.

On 25 July 1950 Lieutenant Colonel L à B Robinson took over the command of the Battalion from Lieutenant Colonel Finch. He was something of a stickler for dress, so that it was a happy coincidence that his take-over was soon followed by the adoption of the blue beret and hose-tops for drill parades and walking-out, a great change for the better. Lest it should be thought that he was a mere parade ground soldier (an illusion that remarkably few people who knew him harboured) he also established the custom of weekly route marches of twenty miles. Very few exceptions were allowed so that many 'employed' men, who had rarely appeared on any except pay parades, suddenly became very conscious of the best friend of the infantrymen, his feet. In view of the forthcoming increase in patrolling this was just as well.

In November came the news that the Battalion had won the Sudan Rifle meeting, a considerable achievement particularly when one takes into account the limited facilities for training.

In December 1950 the United Nations recommended that Eritrea should federate with Ethiopia, a decision which met with little approval, even by the Shifta. An officer serving with the Battalion at the time put it down to the propensity of bureaucrats to decide the fate of millions of people they had never seen by means of small scale maps which they could not read. In view of the situation that prevailed thirty five years later it is difficult to disagree with this assessment.

Meanwhile Shifta activity continued to increase, and patrols hunted them relentlessly. There were few except main roads in the country. Therefore these patrols were necessarily undertaken on foot, out for days at a time and carrying some of their kit on mules as their predecessors had done in Burma. Major successes are hardly to be expected in these circumstances and casualties were received as well as inflicted. Such a case was Corporal Merton, an NCO from The Royal Hampshire Regiment. He was on intelligence duties with the Eritrean Police on 28 July when he and the police travelling in a vehicle with him were ambushed near a police post.

Corporal Merton was killed outright and the policemen were forced to surrender after a desperate fight during which almost all were wounded. Surprisingly enough the Shifta, who numbered thirty-five, contented themselves with robbing the wounded before departing into the friendly hills. A few weeks later the Battalion had its revenge, killing one Shifta, wounding three, and capturing two; and so the deadly game of cat and mouse continued amongst the barren hills.

In the autumn of 1950 the Battalion had to return their Armoured Cars to Ordnance as worn out. The vehicles had been elderly, to say the least, when the Battalion first acquired them and all the care lavished on them could no longer keep them on the road.

The New Year saw no decrease in Shifta activity. On 7 March 1951 a patrol under Lieutenant J.E. Ellis met a band of about thirty of them, and at once engaged them. Lieutenant Ellis was hit in the stomach almost at once, but remained in command until he collapsed from loss of blood. He died in hospital two days later to the regret of all ranks who mourned an active and enterprising officer and a first class sportsman. Anti-Shifta patrols continued almost unceasingly, although the Battalion managed to combine these activities with less warlike matters. These included drill parades (and even a drill competition), preparation for educational certificates, and other mundane but necessary items. Being British soldiers they saw no incongruity in this unlikely mixture of events. The Battalion even ran a flourishing saddle club where all ranks could ride, and occasionally fall off.

On 15 June there occurred a celebrated episode which was to become Regimental (or at least Sergeants' Mess) legend. At about 6 p.m. a Company Commander (who will remain anonymous) was travelling in the Commanding Officer's car with the Paymaster and CSM F. Baston DCM when an armed Shifta crossed the road in front of them. The car stopped to

4. Sgts Ault and Holiday outside the Augustus cinema in Asmara, May 1949. The billboard advertises a boxing match between Lieut Ellis and the Eritrean champion Turco.

allow the Company Commander to engage him with his revolver. However, after two or three misses CSM Baston leant over, took the pistol, and dropped the fleeing Shifta stone dead with a single shot at a very long range indeed. The car following was stopped by a shot in the tyre but at once engaged the remaining bandits of whom they killed a further two and wounded one. All in all it was a most successful little engagement, the only casualty being the Paymaster who was slightly wounded in the wrist.

In June 1951 all ranks were much heartened by a message from HM King George VI, relayed through the Colonel of the Regiment which read.

'His Majesty has been watching the reports of conditions in Eritrea for some months, and is fully aware of the trying condition in that area. He would be glad if you would let the Commanding Officer and all ranks know how much he appreciates the way in which they are standing up to their difficulties and maintaining the high reputation of the Regiment.'

As it happened the Battalion's bandit hunting days were almost over (at least in Eritrea), for on 29 July a warning order was received to move to Cyprus.

Just before they went, a general amnesty was announced and, rather to everyone's surprise, the great bulk of the Shifta bands took advantage of it. On the day appointed for the ceremony, which took place at a hilltop monastery outside the town, hundreds of Shifta were assembled, still fully armed, before the official British delegation arrived. The officer representing the Battalion remembers his feelings as he climbed the hillside under the interested gaze of his erstwhile enemies, but in the event all went peacefully. Amongst those who came in was an old and notorious opponent, one Geremedin Kefela, the leader of the band which had been responsible for the death of John Ellis earlier in the year. He was quite an affable character, and extremely proud of the fact that he had been trained as an irregular against the Italians by Orde Wingate in 1940.

After a short postponement the Battalion finally sailed for Cyprus on 24 August 1951. It left behind it a country largely free of Shifta and could justifiably be proud of the vital role it had played in bringing about this happy state of affairs.

2 Egypt and Colchester

When the Battalion arrived in Cyprus there was no trouble and it settled down to enjoy the luxury of peace-time routine in pleasant surroundings; although many found it quiet after the fleshpots of Asmara. Unfortunately this peaceful interlude was not to last long, for on 20 October 1951 the Battalion embarked at Famagusta for Egypt, where they disembarked at Port Said on 22 March. This emergency move was dictated mainly by the abrogation by the Egyptian Parliament of the Anglo-Egyptian Treaty of 1936. This Treaty, the implementation of which had been long delayed by the Second World War, agreed on the evacuation by the British of the whole of the country except for the Suez Canal, which it was considered essential to retain. Its abrogation on 15 October had made it clear that the Egyptian Government wanted the British out altogether.

After a period spent in a transit camp the Battalion moved to Kabrit and then to El Ballah, the move to the last place being complete by 18 November.

On 18 December came the first clear indication of the changed mood of the Egyptian people. Three private soldiers in the Battalion, no doubt lulled into a sense of false security by the relative safety of Asmara and Famagusta, strayed into an out of bounds area near Ismailia Station and were at once attacked viciously by a mob of infuriated Egyptians. Two of the soldiers, who were unarmed, were so badly hacked about that they were dead on arrival at hospital, while the third, although badly hurt, made a good recovery.

The situation deteriorated steadily thereafter, and life quickly reverted to the familiar routine of road patrols and endless guards which had been the lot of the Battalion for as long as anyone serving with it could remember. At least the fresh supply of drafts enabled A Company to be reformed, which went some way towards easing the situation. It was hard for anyone to feel much Christmas spirit and such festivities as were possible had to be spread over four days.

On 12 January 1952 the Battalion moved its base to Golf Course Camp, Port Said, in relief of 1st Battalion The Cheshire Regiment. Only Battalion Headquarters, B Company, and Headquarter Company were in the camp itself; A Company being at El Raswa, C Company at 156 Transit Camp, and D Company at the docks.

On the night of 18/19 January Golf Course Camp came under scattered rifle fire. Although it lasted for some time the shooting was random and no casualties were sustained. However, the Egyptian Press reported later that no fewer than forty-one soldiers had been killed and sixty-two wounded. The Battalion accepted these purely paper figures with composure. Occasional sniping continued for some days until towards the end of January the Commanding Officer ordered a 17 pounder anti-tank gun to open fire on Port Said station. No record appears to exist of the number of rounds expended, but the Egyptian papers reported that naval guns had been used, weapons which they appeared to regard as extremely unsporting.

On 15 February memorial services were held for his late Majesty King George VI, who had become Colonel-in-Chief of the Regiment only five years previously.

In spite of its wide dispersal the Battalion somehow contrived to hold two RSM drill parades each week. Signals exercises, lectures, and some sport also took place, although they were necessarily to some extent improvised. Tofrek Day was celebrated, but because of the recent death of the Colonel-in-Chief proceedings were kept low key.

The Battalion moved to Suez in April, where it remained under canvas in Copenhagen Camp, adjacent to the Suez Bowl, as part of 2 Brigade. C Company was detached to Kabrit for six weeks, erecting a leave camp by the side of Lake Timsah.

On 5 June all ranks were delighted to hear that the Commanding Officer, Lieutenant Colonel Robinson had been awarded a well-earned OBE in HM Queen Elizabeth's first honours list. Six days later he commanded the Queen's Birthday Parade, a company of the Battalion being included in the parade troops under his command. On 1 July A Company was again disbanded through lack of manpower.

On 5 July there was a military coup. King Farouk abdicated in favour of his son, and very sensibly left the country as soon as possible thereafter. Although an ominous development in the longer term, this led to something of a lull, so that other activities were able to be resumed. In November the Battalion took part in various exercises, Exercise Triangles being the most important. They also won the Brigade Rifle Meeting, but had to be content with second place in the Divisional one. The year concluded with the usual Christmas festivities, which were not unduly interrupted by operational requirements.

On 14 March the Advance Party left for England, to the cautious delight of the Battalion, who had seen such false starts before. This time however there were no hitches, and less than a month later the Battalion started on its way. It did not depart without elements of farce which seems to be inseparable from service in Egypt. After extensive delays due to a power cable across the line, the Battalion was finally pulling away from a long-disused halt (mysteriously, but aptly, renamed 'Robbie's Halt' during the night) to a vigorous rendering of 'Take me back to Dear Old Blighty' by the band of the Cheshires. Suddenly it was discovered that the Colour Party had been left behind, so the train had to be shunted back to enable the Colour Party to clamber on with as much dignity as they could muster. Then, in a siding in Port Said, the train was surrounded by swarms of hawkers of various food and drinks who, in spite of their current dislike of the British, were certainly not loath to do business with them. In order to disperse them, a particularly savage alsatian dog was let loose amongst them. Unfortunately its first victim was the train's engine driver who, having climbed down from his cab in all innocence, promptly sustained a nasty bite on his calf. The Battalion then embarked on

5. The Canal Zone, 1951–53. 'Robbie's Halt'. The hastily constructed entraining point for the 1st Battalion's departure from Suez. Copenhagen Camp and the main Suez–Cairo road is in the background.

6. The Coronation Year 1953.
The 1st Battalion's Colour
Party for the 2 June.
L to R: Maj Hill, Cpl Watkiss,
Sgt Crockford, Lt Herman
(Queen's Colour),
C/Sgt Llewellyn, Lt Paxton
(Regimental Colour),
Sgt Hooks, Pte Turner,
RSM Harrington-Jones.

HMT Empire Clyde on 13 April to be met at Liverpool by a reception committee headed by the Colonel of the Regiment. It had been absent continuously from the United Kingdom for just over nineteen and a half years, a period which included the Second World War during which it had played a distinguished part in its then capacity as the 2nd Battalion.

On 2 June 1953 a party of six officers and forty-seven other ranks, under the command of Major L.J.L. Hill MC, took part in the Coronation of HM Queen Elizabeth II, while the remainder of the Battalion was still on disembarkation leave. The three weeks prior to the Coronation were in themselves a campaign to prepare for the parade. The marching contingent was required to march ten abreast with the Colours in the centre and also to split and rejoin through Marble Arch. Almost the whole 15 miles of the route was marched 'to attention' and at the slope. The endurance and precision needed for officers with swords, ensigns with the Colours and the escort with rifles was immense. Training was carried out both by a series of 20 mile route marches along the roads of Essex in the early morning and on the square, where a mock up of Marble Arch was erected, under the direction of RSM Harrington-Jones. The Colours were carried by Lieutenants Herman and Paxton. The party's duty ended on 8th June, on which date the whole unit re-assembled at Roman Way Camp, Colchester.

On 15 June D Company moved to Buckenham Tofts Camp, north of Thetford, to erect a tented camp for the Battalion from where it would run the Eastern Command Territorial and Cadet summer camps. Needless to say it rained continuously and heavily throughout these preliminary proceedings, which did not exactly make for comfort. D Company was followed by the remainder of the Battalion, less A Company and the bulk of HQ Company, a week later, having run the East Anglian Rifle Meeting in the interval. The description of Buckenham Tofts Camp which appeared later in the *China Dragon* (although apparently written by someone without much regard for the Game Laws), is far too apt not to be reproduced verbatim, especially since it will inevitably be recognised as substantially true by anyone in the British Army who knew it at that period:

> 'We found Buckenham Tofts to consist of a large, derelict house, almost entirely surrounded by trees and rabbits (this it should be noted was just before the days of mixomatosis). Unfortunately for our countrymen the most stringent provisions of both military and civil law were evoked against anyone who so much as offered a cross word at a passing pheasant, so that any rosy visions of mass slaughter of the local game were strangled at birth. A small river ran through the estate but although the authorities had not arranged to patrol it with a gun-boat, every available tree carried threats of ex-communication, slow torture, and the Death of a Thousand Cuts, against any malefactor dipping an unsanctioned hook into its sacred waters.'

To anyone with experience of Berkshire (and perhaps particularly Royal Berkshire) poachers it is difficult to believe that these tempting coverts remained completely unscathed. However, as one important requirement of anyone indulging in the pastime is discretion, we shall probably never know.

On 1 July Lieutenant Colonel C.L. Speers assumed command of the Battalion from Lieutenant Colonel Robinson, just in time for the first onslaught of the Territorial Army, which happily included the 4th/6th Battalion under Lieutenant Colonel P.H.C. Hayward. After them came a second wave from the Combined Cadet Forces. The day after Maiwand found the Battalion surrounded as far as the eye could see by cadets of all ages, sizes, and conditions. As darkness descended the confused sounds of numerous contingent bands, all in apparent competition with each other and punctuated by occasional yelling and massed cheering, made the Battalion briefly imagine that it was in an Afghan encampment of seventy-three years earlier. In the event all went extremely well and the General Officer Commanding Eastern Command, Lieutenant General G.K. Bourne CB CMG CBE issued a most appreciative order of the day as a result.

In the midst of all their work, hard and often dirty as it was, the Battalion still had time to marvel at the quantity of food consumed, especially by the Army Cadet Force. In spite of four, more than adequate, meals each day one camp managed to consume two tons of chocolate in a period of ten days.

In the early autumn the Battalion ceased its housekeeping and, having dismantled all the TA camps in the area, were shortly afterwards concentrated at West Tofts Camp where it was at last able to do some rather belated training on its own account. Two battalion exercises, one on the occupation of a hastily prepared defensive position, the other concerned with the advance to contact and a battalion attack, did much to brush up tactics and procedures. At their end the Battalion returned to Colchester, where it finally concentrated at the beginning of November.

Bourlon Wood was fully celebrated by a series of social and sporting events, at one of which, an All Ranks dance, the NAAFI actually ran out of beer. Whether this was due to excessive consumption or a simple miscalculation on the part of the NAAFI is not known. Fortunately the Sergeants' Mess, to whom such a mishap was unthinkable, came to the rescue with further supplies, which saved the day.

At about this time the Commanding Officer was officially informed that the Battalion was to go to BAOR in April 1954. This was a welcome move, since it at least offered a two years' accompanied tour in comfortable surroundings.

Christmas saw the usual celebrations, although as the Battalion was in England most people were understandably anxious to spend it at home. Most of the official functions, including a large children's party to which the families of the Devonshire Regiment and the Gloucestershire Regiments (both of which were serving abroad) were also invited, were thus completed early, after which the bulk of the Battalion went on leave on Christmas Eve. The Battalion reassembled in the New Year. At once it became involved with range work and individual and section training, while the Support Platoons, the Signal Platoon, and the MT Platoon carried out instructional cadres. This was all in preparation for the Battalion's new role in BAOR, where it was to form part of the Lorried Infantry Brigade of an Armoured Division.

The weather was far from kind, February in particular being foul in every respect, but the Battalion persevered and much valuable preliminary training for its new role was achieved.

In spite of pressure of work the Battalion won the East Anglian District Cross Country on 23 January but only achieved fourth place at the Eastern Command competition on 23 February. By this time the move was getting near and so much work was underway that no holiday was granted for Tofrek Day. The first advance party of five officers and one hundred other ranks had already left on 13 March, and was followed by a second, much smaller one on 30 March. Over the 25–26 March the Colonel of the Regiment paid his farewell visit. On 4 April 1954 the main body embarked at Harwich for the Hook of Holland and then travelled by rail to its final destination, which it reached on the evening of 5 April.

3 Goslar

Goslar turned out to be a most attractive old town. It was surrounded on three sides by spurs of the Harz Mountains and not far from Bad Harzburg, a well known tourist area which then included a Rhine Army leave centre. Goslar had not apparently been damaged in the war and, being a tourist town, was used to foreigners of all kinds, particularly Danes who visited the place in large numbers. The latter were great admirers of the British, and as soon as it was announced they were in town every available subaltern had urgent business there.

The barrack area, once a Luftwaffe station, was set amongst pine woods and covered a vast area, so large indeed that the November 1954 issue of the China Dragon states that it was a quarter of an hour's march from A Company to Battalion Headquarters. It adds that soldiers in close arrest covered the distance in a considerably shorter time. Some of the families were in large flats in barracks, but the bulk were in furnished houses in the town itself, a couple of miles away. The buildings, particularly perhaps the messes, were large and comfortably – indeed almost palatially – furnished and equipped. The whole barracks was staffed by a most efficient body of German civilians.

The Battalion found itself in 91st Lorried Infantry Brigade of 11th Armoured Division. Mobility was of course essential when operating with tanks and in the 1950's this was provided by wheeled troop-carrying vehicles, usually known as TCVs, which were a slightly modified version of the standard 3 tonner and were driven by Royal Army Service Corps personnel. These vehicles, each carrying a platoon, were trundled round the countryside in broad daylight, in the hopes apparently, that in the event of war the allies would have air superiority. It must of course be remembered that the Russians only just succeeded at that time in producing a prototype hydrogen bomb.

After a short settling-in period the Battalion started a period of training at low level which included signals and administrative exercises, the former being of particular importance in an Armoured division where reliable communications were of particular importance. On 11 May the Battalion moved to Sennelager for field firing. This training was of great practical value and the Battalion benefited greatly from it. The ranges were staffed entirely by elderly German civilians, most being of pre-war vintage, who had the business down to a fine art. Concealed targets appeared and disappeared amidst bursts of blank firing by machine guns hidden in pits, the whole thing being worked by miles of concealed signal cable. Much historical interest was added by the fact that it was of pre-war origin and Hitler was reputed to have watched his panzer divisions exercising from the top of a nearby tower. This was followed by a stay at a tented camp where Company and Battalion level training, followed by a brigade exercise, put the Battalion into good shape for the larger scale exercises of 1955.

In May details of the Battalion affiliated units were announced; they consisted of No 1 (Bulls) Battery, 2 RHA, the 9th Lancers, C Company, 1st Battalion Kings Royal Rifle Corps (Motor Battalion) and B Platoon 54 Company Royal Army Service Corps which provided drivers for the TCVs.

On 10 July the Battalion was again in Sennelager, this time for a ceremonial parade to mark the visit of HRH Princess Margaret. The event was a success, although marred by heavy rain.

Due to an exercise, Maiwand Day could not be celebrated at the proper time, but time was found later on 14–16 August. In September a change in officers dress took place by the adoption of the Queen's pattern cap badge.

The training season was by then over and, on 9 November, this fact was marked by the Annual Administrative Inspection. It was carried out by the Divisional Commander, who expressed himself as very satisfied with the state of the Battalion.

Christmas followed with the usual festivities. Unlike the previous year, where being in England most people had gone on leave, the whole Battalion was in station so that events could follow the traditional pattern.

On 10 January 1955 came the welcome news that the Machine Gun Platoon had won the BAOR Cup, a notable feat against strong opposition whilst on 1st February the Battalion also won the Brigade Boxing, a feat they quickly followed up on 4 March by also winning the BAOR quarter-finals in Berlin. They were finally beaten in the semi-finals on 25 March by the Lancashire Fusiliers, after a close and hard fought contest.

On 16 March the Colonel of the Regiment visited the Battalion where he was received by a Guard of Honour. A guest night was held the same evening and was attended by a number of senior officers from 1 (British) Corps. Next evening he visited the Sergeants' Mess for the Tofrek Ball which had been brought forward a few days to coincide with his visit. He had such a full itinerary that he had to leave the Ball at 1 am and go straight onto the aircraft taking him home.

7. The Colonel of the Regiment presenting the Machine Gun platoon trophy to Lt Tremellen, March 1955.

On 18 April the Battalion returned to Sennelager for field firing, and once again they received great benefit from it. On the first day or so the clouds of dust thrown up by the Bren guns caused continual stoppages but by the end of the week the Number Ones had improved out of all recognition. By then the Battalion had become accustomed to high standards of messing and was somewhat surprised to find that in this respect Sennelager by no means reached the high standards of Goslar. The individual at that time responsible for compiling the Digest of Service also refers with obvious disdain to 'the establishment known as B Mess'. So, the officers suffered too. Whilst at Sennelager all ranks went into shirtsleeve order, which inevitably caused it to snow quite heavily that same morning.

On 5 May the ratification of the Bonn Treaty meant that troops in BAOR were no longer classed as 'on active service', which made little practical difference except that German civil courts could now try British soldiers for civil offences. This led to dire threats regarding the severity with which motoring offences would in future be punished, but in the event made little difference.

After almost three weeks at Sennelager the Battalion moved to Soltau for higher formation training, which included river crossings. The area had little to commend it except that the soil was light which made digging easy, quite a consideration when the Battalion had to dig in deeply with overhead cover against the possibility of nuclear attack.

One distinct advantage of the place was its proximity to Hamburg with its notorious Reeperbahn, the proximity of which all ranks took full advantage.

8. Goslar (BAOR) 1953–6. The 1st Battalion marches through Hanover after the Queen's Birthday Parade on 9 June 1955. Colour Party: Lts Tremellen and Redding, RSM Baston DCM. Company Commanders: Major Myatt MC and Capt Blascheck MC

Even the company commanders ventured there in a body, and although they were all normally grave and responsible individuals these traits were less in evidence as the evening progressed. The 1st Battalion editorial in the China Dragon makes vaguely disproving reference to certain episodes. Amongst them was one concerning a camel and another a bubble bath, but does not go into further details; a sensible decision which the present writer proposes to follow.

On 31 May the Battalion, less D Company, having been selected for the Queens Birthday Parade, moved to Hanover and started rehearsing intensively for the occasion which took place on 9 June. The parade day turned out to be dry and sunny and the parade at which the salute was taken by Major General J.D'A. Anderson CBE DSO GOC 11th Armoured Division, and commanded by the Commanding Officer, Lieutenant Colonel Speers, was a great success. It took place in the presence of a large and appreciative audience, largely German, most of whom apparently had babies in arms with them. The result was that when the Battalion fired a feu-de-joie, and a very good one too, an unearthly wail was heard all over the arena, a wail subsequently exceeded when 'Bulls Troop' 2 RHA started firing their salute. Due to the absence of the Regimental Band at another ceremony, music for the occasion was provided by the bands of 13th/18th Hussars and the 1st Battalion The Border Regiment.

The parade was followed by a march through Hanover with bayonets fixed, Colours flying, and the Band and Drums playing. This, too, was received enthusiastically by the locals, the only cause for uneasiness being the mounted

9. The Freedom of Abingdon, 29 June 1955. D Company, seen here marching past the Mayor and Corporation, represented the 1st Battalion.

German police who accompanied the Colours. The horses were by no means accustomed to martial music at close quarters and their riders, not all of whom appeared to be very secure in their saddles, had the greatest difficulty in controlling them. At times indeed there was almost the need to form square, but in the event it never quite came to that.

The absence from the scene of D Company was due to the fact that they were required to attend the parade at Abingdon marking the Granting of the Freedom of Entry of the Borough to the Regiment. The ceremony took place at 7p.m. on 29 June. Proceedings in the Corn Exchange were opened by the presentation by the Mayor of a Scroll, a Casket, and a Silver Bugle to the Colonel of the Regiment, to which the latter made a suitable reply. The Mayor then inspected a detachment of the Regiment consisting of D Company, a company of the 4th/6th Battalion, and the Band of the 1st Battalion, under command of Major R.B.G. Bromhead MBE, the Second-in-Command of the 1st Battalion. The Colours of both Battalions were on parade. The 1st Battalion Colours had also been on the Hanover parade, after which they had been flown to England, complete with their Colour Party, to take part in the second ceremony. After the inspection the parade marched through the town with the Colours flying, bayonets fixed, and band playing in the traditional way, the salute being taken by the Mayor. The route at the saluting base was lined by a detachment of the Royal Berkshires under Lieutenant Colonel D.C.S. Sinclair OBE, a retired regular officer of the Regiment, the day being closed by an all ranks dance in the Corn Exchange.

In spite of a busy programme of training and ceremonial the Battalion also had a good record in sport. On 25 June it won the Brigade Athletics Championship by a wide margin, and two days later was equally successful in the Divisional meeting although by a much narrower margin. On 15 July the BAOR Meeting resulted in a fourth place only, but CSMI Cleaver APTC, who was largely responsible for the Battalion's earlier successes, won the discus. A few days later he not only succeeded in winning the same event in the BAOR Individuals but broke his earlier Army record with a remarkable throw of 142 feet 4 inches.

Despite a limited season the Battalion also did well at cricket, winning the Divisional Championship and being narrowly beaten by the Cheshires in the BAOR quarter finals. The team also performed creditably in a number of other matches.

The anniversary of Maiwand saw the usual festivities including a magnificent ball in the Sergeants' Mess at which the officers wore mess kit for the first time since 1939. A fête arranged for 23 July had to be postponed until 29 due to heavy rain, but was then a great success and enjoyed by all concerned. The possible exception was the unfortunate pig, which was given as a prize for the traditional bowling, but whose eventual fate has not been recorded, which in all the circumstances is perhaps just as well.

Exercises of all kinds continued throughout the summer and the Battalion acquitted itself well in all of them. A new phonetic alphabet came into use on 10 August which caused some initial difficulties amongst the more mature

10. 1956, Warrant Officers
and Sergeants of the 1st
Battalion with the Colonel
of the Regiment.

officers, many of who had only just succeeded in mastering the old one.
Communications were so vital in an Armoured division however that it had
to be mastered and it quickly was, with some assistance from a uniformly
excellent signal platoon, who being young were much more adaptable than
some of the seniors.

It may not be out of place to discuss here the general state of the Regiment
ten years after the end of the Second World War. Like other line regiments
its only regular units consisted of a single battalion and a depot. In spite of
this limited commitment the officers' roll still showed a total (excluding
Quartermasters) of sixty regular officers of whom 2 were Lieutenant
Colonels, 37 were Majors, 10 were Captains, and 13 were Subalterns. There
were a further 26 short-service officers, none above the rank of Major and
mostly Captains and Subalterns, as well as 18 National Service Officers. The
majority of these were of course employed on the staff or at other extra-
regimental jobs. Even so the Battalion was much over-strength in field
officers and lamentably short of Captains. Although this situation apparently
offered hopes for the future, it actually reduced the prospects of most Majors
to vanishing point. It was, even then, becoming apparent that some reduc-
tions were inevitable. However, when a major reorganisation came a couple of
years later it was, as we shall see, on a scale that few, if any, can have envis-
aged. In spite of these forebodings for the future, morale remained very high
as these pages clearly show, a fact largely due to the personality of the Commanding Officer, who, although he could be tough if necessary, usually ran
the Battalion with a light sure touch. Among his many virtues was his willing-
ness to leave his company commanders, who were all very experienced, to
get on with things with only the necessary minimum of supervision.

11. General Sir Miles Dempsey accompanied by the Commanding Officer, Lt Col Speers, inspect the Band and Drums during a visit in April 1956. The Colonel of the Regiment's ADC is Lt Dunn.

On 4 November the Battalion heard that it could expect to return to the United Kingdom in May or June 1956, and thence go to Malaya in late 1956 or early 1957. The prospect on the whole was attractive, not only because of the stay in England, but because the Royal Berkshire Regiment had not before served in Malaya. There was an emergency there to be sure, but then there were emergencies everywhere. In any case this particular one, which was of many years duration, was more or less on its last legs.

Winter 1955 saw the continuation of border patrols along the western side of the high wire fences and minefields, with their ominous watch towers, erected by the East German regime. West Germany had recently been permitted to establish its own guards in the form of the 'Bundesgrenzschutz', with whom we were to co-operate. Skiing was taught to all ranks and patrols were carried out on skis. The Battalion learnt the meaning of frostbite, how to avoid it while exercising in temperatures down to minus 30 degrees and how to live in snow igloos for long periods.

Then came Christmas with all its festivities, and no sooner was that over than on 12 January 1956 came the incredible news that the Machine Gun Platoon had won the BAOR cup for the second successive year. At the end of the same month came the equally glad news that the Battalion was to receive new colours from Her Majesty the Queen at Windsor on 17 July. On the basis that good things always come in threes, there also came the news that Her Majesty had honoured the Colonel of the Regiment with the Order of Knight Grand Cross of the British Empire. The Battalion also heard that he was soon to relinquish the Colonelcy. Brigadier Hogg, a universally popular choice, would replace him.

Winter routine continued. On 23 February the Commanding Officer once again demonstrated his delightful sense of humour by sending two of his company commanders on a Christian leadership course. Although not previously famed for their religious ardour they accepted with resignation, to the unconcealed joy of the subalterns.

On 3 April General Sir Miles and Lady Dempsey visited the Battalion for a few days to celebrate its departure from BAOR. He was received by a Guard of Honour found by C Company. His time thereafter was taken up by a round of festivities, culminating in a most magnificent Ball at which almost everyone who was anyone in BAOR was present. All the officers were in Mess kit, that of the Colonel of the Regiment being the same one he had last worn as a Lieutenant Colonel seventeen years before. He had omitted to add a second star on his tunic which prompted one guest to remark in awe-struck tones that he had never before seen such a distinguished commanding officer.

On 13 April the Advance Party left for Assaye Barracks at Tidworth and three days later that of the Bedfordshire and Hertfordshire Regiment arrived to take over the barracks in Goslar. On 16 May, by coincidence the anniversary of the Battle of Albuhera in 1811, the main body of the Battalion, including families, left BAOR and were soon settling into their new home.

4 UK and Malta

On arrival in Tidworth the Battalion went on leave in two parties but had reassembled by 5 June 1956. There followed a short period of settling in and by 27 June rehearsals for the presentation of new colours were in full swing. On 13 July the new colours were put on display outside the guardroom, and three days later the Battalion moved by special train to Windsor where they were accommodated in Victoria Barracks, their hosts being the 3rd Battalion the Grenadier Guards. Due to lack of accommodation the officers were put up in the very comfortable Castle Hotel overlooking the river, a most civilised arrangement.

The morning of the parade, 21 July, brought fairly menacing cloud, and everyone was apprehensive. There were no weather satellites in those days, but the RAF Meteorological report was favourable, and as it turned out, accurate, with no rain falling. Every last detail had been checked and rechecked, and all that remained to do was to carry everything out as rehearsed. At ten o'clock the Adjutant reported to the Commanding Officer that the parade was correct and the Battalion moved off. At twenty minutes past ten the ground keepers took up position on the East Terrace, followed by the Quartermaster's party with the new colours, still of course cased. At ten thirty five the Battalion marched on and a few minutes later greeted the Colonel of the Regiment with a General Salute. There followed the Troop and the moving ceremony of marching off the old colours, which had seen much service since their presentation in 1907. At three minutes past eleven Her Majesty arrived and carried out the ceremony of presenting the new colours. The Colours, now uncased, were handed by the field officers to Her Majesty who in turn gave them to the ensigns, kneeling to receive them. The Queen then addressed the parade and the Commanding Officer replied. Then the Battalion formed column of guards and marched past to the 'Dashing White Sergeant'. It then turned into line, and gave Her Majesty a Royal Salute followed by three cheers, which signalled the end of the parade.

The Queen then walked along the line of spectators before moving to the officers' tent, where the officers and their wives were presented. Lieutenant Colonel Charles Speers then presented Her Majesty with a badge in diamonds and rubies and expressed the hope that 'your Majesty may be pleased sometime to wear the China Dragon'. Prince Charles and Princess Anne, then of course small children, were also present, and the Prince, whilst admiring the Regimental Silver, found some snuff in one of the boxes. After explanations as to its purpose and properties he turned to an equerry and invited him to give a demonstration. The young man blanched but complied, with results that delighted the young Prince.

After photographs with the officers and sergeants Her Majesty left and everyone was free to join their friends and talk. The author makes no apology for describing these events at some length, for not only was it a unique occasion for the Regiment, the presentation of new colours to a regular Battalion by the Monarch in the ancient stronghold of the British Monarchy, but also as it turned out, the last great piece of ceremony in which the Royal Berkshire Regiment ever took part.

Order of Parade for the
Presentation of New Colours to
The Royal Berkshire Regiment by
Her Majesty the Queen
21 July 1956

Commanding Officer: Lieutenant Colonel C.L. Speers
Field Officer to Her Majesty The Queen: Major F.D. Jones MC
Officers for the Colours
Old Colour   New Colour
Lieut J.P. Ward   Lieut L.C. Tremellen
2/Lieut J.M. Morris   Lieut J.D. Redding

Adjutant
Major T.C.S. Jennings

Quarter-Master
Lieut (QM) H. Green DCM

No. 1 Guard
Major R.B.C. Bromhead MBE
Lieut D.C. Murray
CSM E. Leadbetter

No. 2 Guard
Capt P.D. Newman
Lieut P.T. Dunn
Lieut J.E. Rogers
CSM H. Pearson

No. 3 Guard
Major C.M. Tuffill
Lieut J.A.H. Macmillan
2/Lieut C.B. Smallbone
CSM R. Mitchell

No. 4 Guard
Major F. Myatt MC
Lieut R.M.C. Wilson
2/Lieut M. Barnes
CSM S. Llewellyn

Regimental Sergeant Major: F. Baston DCM
Band Master: W. Freeth
Drum Major: W. Choules

12. The Suez Crisis – 1956. August and the 1st Battalion descend on Malta for training and to await events. The seashore camp of Bahar-i-Caghar (where this photo was taken) was their home for the next two months.

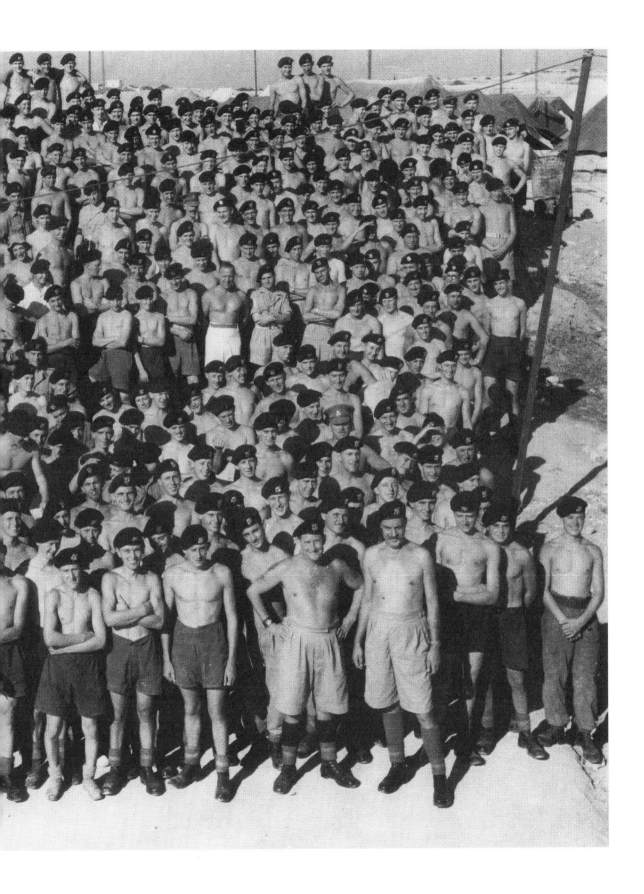

27 UK and Malta

13. The Anti-Tank Platoon was attached to 40 Commando RM for the operation. A section is seen here in a suburb of Port Said. Note the dismounted 106mm recoilless rifle, which was rushed into service for the operation. The carrier is a turretless Stuart light tank.

After the Colour Parade the Battalion dispersed to undertake the traditional task of a regular battalion in the United Kingdom, the running of the summer camps for the Territorial Army and Cadets. These were to be followed by guards of honour for the Queen at Abingdon and Wallingford, plus various marches round the county before the Battalion departed for Malaya. In the meanwhile farewells were said to Lieutenant Colonel Speers who on 22 July handed over command to Lieutenant Colonel Bromhead who, though no one knew it at the time, was to have the melancholy distinction of being the last officer to command a regular battalion of the Royal Berkshire Regiment. Afterwards the Battalion prepared to resume normal routine.

The posting to the Far East had been confirmed a few days earlier in a confidential letter from the War Office announcing the date and destination for the move, which gave the Battalion some seven months to prepare for it. This was not at all unexpected, since the old pre-war Indian contractor of the 2nd Battalion, who had extended the scope of his operations to cover Malaya, had already given the same information.

Then on 1 August came the announcement that the Battalion was to be on immediate readiness to go to an unknown destination, an abrupt change of plan made necessary by the deterioration of the Egyptian situation. There followed a period of frenetic activity, for the Battalion had to be reassembled and the bulk of the National Servicemen replaced because they lacked enough residual Colour service to be eligible. Khaki drill had to be drawn and issued, together with a great variety of other stores, and a hundred and one other tasks completed, including the absorption of fifty rather dazed regular reservists who had been plucked from civil life with the minimum of warning. The newly appointed brigade commander, who arrived at this moment by helicopter to address a largely non-existent Battalion, was horrified, and gave it as his opinion that many of the Battalion would go absent. Events soon proved him wrong, for when the deadline came the Battalion was present with the exception of one lance corporal, who turned up two days later, having crashed his motorcycle in his haste to get back.

In spite of the short notice all was ready in time, and over the period 12–16 August 1956 the Battalion flew out from Hurn airport in BOAC Britannias to the 'unknown destination', which finally turned out to be Malta.

The Battalion was accommodated near St Paul's Bay at the Northern part of the island, the exact spot being Bahar-i-Caghar (the final part being pronounced 'char') which was the site of a summer camp of the Royal Malta Artillery. The accommodation, which consisted of 160lb tents, with a few larger ones for messes and stores, was spartan but adequate and all ranks soon settled in. The first real need was to acclimatise the troops by gradual exposure to the sun, while instituting an intensive course of basic training to bring the numerous drafts up to the standard necessary for active operations, which seemed likely to start shortly. Malta is small and highly cultivated, and with at least ten other major units on the island, training areas were at an absolute premium. Fortunately adequate ranges were available and the soldiers were further hardened up by route marches round the island. By starting at about 6 p.m. this both afforded the advantage of cool weather, with the further advantage that the soldiers got a night's sleep and were thus fit for an early start next morning.

The officers were accommodated in a large, typically Maltese building on a small headland a few yards from the sea. It was believed to have once been a house of ill repute, but whatever its antecedents the building proved adequate for its present use. A large vine-shaded courtyard provided space for a very reasonable restaurant, run by an ex-Mess Sergeant of the Kings Own Malta Regiment, not two hundred yards distant. There was good swimming nearby and the bright lights to suit all tastes in Valetta, a few miles away. The Drums took the opportunity to beat retreat one evening, and as the numerous spectators were generous with return invitations, social life was well provided for.

On 3 September the Anti-Tank platoon was attached to 40 Commando Royal Marines (who had no heavy anti-tank guns of their own) in anticipation of an assault landing in Egypt. The platoon was originally equipped with 17 pounders which, although very effective, were large and clumsy pieces. However, two detachments had been re-equipped with 106mm recoilless guns, which were much more portable.

On 6 November the two detachments of 106's went in with the first wave, while the four remaining detachments followed with their 17 pounders in the second. No tanks were encountered, but the platoon, much harassed by snipers from the surrounding roofs, finally replied with their heavier metal, which not only eliminated the first rifleman but also blew the entire dome of the building to smithereens. Having once established the effectiveness of their action they continued to use it thereafter, to the comfort of both the platoon and the Marines accompanying them. On 14 November the Battalion received a signal from Brigadier R.W. Madoc commanding 3 Commando Brigade which read:

'I wish to express my appreciation of the splendid fighting
qualities of your Anti-Tank platoon which we were privileged
to have with us during the Amphibious Assault of Port Said.
They were invaluable to us and it is a great privilege to
have them with us'.

By the time the platoon rejoined the Battalion the latter had had another move. They were the only members of the Battalion to be awarded the General Service Medal with the bar 'Near East'.

One indication of their acceptance by the Royal Marines was the fact that they were invited to adopt the familiar black belts worn by the latter, an invitation which needless to say was quickly accepted.

On 26 September the Commanding Officer assembled the Battalion and informed them that they could expect to move shortly to the usual 'unknown destination' and on 7 October they embarked from Valetta on *HMT Parkestone* for the next leg of their journey which was soon revealed to be Cyprus. Two days later they had disembarked at Limassol, on the south coast of the island.

5 Cyprus – The End

Cyprus, an Eastern Mediterranean island about half as large as Wales, had been ceded to Britain by Turkey, not without the application of some pressure, in 1878 as a base from which the Suez route to India might be defended if necessary. In 1954, as a result of the negotiations for the British evacuation of Egypt, it was announced that Middle East Headquarters were to be moved to the island, a decision that soon led to trouble. The population was largely Greek with a considerable minority, amounting to about 20 per cent of the whole, of Turks. Although the two communities had lived in reasonable amity for many years there was a long standing wish on the part of the Greeks for union with Greece, a movement perhaps better known as 'Enosis'.

The establishment of the new Headquarters on the island was intended to make it clear to the local inhabitants that there was little chance of achieving their objectives. This stance was reinforced by the Foreign Office which, although prepared to offer a high degree of internal self government, made it quite clear that it was not prepared to countenance any change of sovereignty.

The Greek majority was largely under the influence of the Greek Orthodox Church, led by the ambitious Archbishop Makarios. The church had a say in affairs almost incredible to those who did not actually witness it, insisting on its claim for union with Greece. Greece was also very much in

14. Cyprus 1956–59. Anti-Eoka operations. The Battalion moved from Malta to Cyprus in October to a hastily erected camp at Episkopi, minus two companies at Dhekhelia. The site, known as Happy Valley, later became an outdoor sporting complex for Episkopi garrison. The photograph was taken from the area of new Paramali officers' married quarters.

favour of the movement, so much so that it not only set up a guerrilla organisation, usually known as Eoka, but also provided a leader for it in the person of George Grivas, an ex-colonel in the Greek regular army. Ample funds were provided through the medium of the church. Once established, Eoka made good progress. Its first, classical step being the neutralisation of the police; the latter, being of the Greek Orthodox Church, were already very much under the influence of the priests, and any recalcitrants were soon brought to heel by means of threats to their families.

Despite precautionary measures, extra troops were sent to Cyprus from August 1954 onwards. There was no real hostility towards them until December of that year. This was when the United Nations General Assembly finally rejected Greece's claim to the island, after which an open revolt developed.

The situation continued with increasing gravity, and although more and more troops were made available from elsewhere, things did not improve. This was the situation when 1st Battalion The Royal Berkshire Regiment arrived in October 1956.

Its first camp was on the south coast at Happy Valley near Episkopi and did not, in the circumstances, inspire much confidence in the more experienced members of the Battalion. The camp was in a narrow valley closely commanded by hills on all sides, and with a perimeter consisting of single coils of dannert wire, through which the numerous goats grazing in the vicinity passed with disconcerting ease. At this time A and B Companies were detached to Dhekhelia, some seventy miles further east. Although the Greek population was conspicuously absent the Battalion was cheered by the appearance of a representative of the same ubiquitous firm of Indian contractors which the 2nd Battalion had dealt with in India before the War, and who professed himself and his minions ready to look after everything.

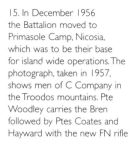

15. In December 1956 the Battalion moved to Primasole Camp, Nicosia, which was to be their base for island wide operations. The photograph, taken in 1957, shows men of C Company in the Troodos mountains. Pte Woodley carries the Bren followed by Ptes Coates and Hayward with the new FN rifle

In view of the continuance of the Suez crisis the Commanding Officer left the island on 26 October for a reconnaissance on the North African coast, being followed a few days later by a small advance party.

On 3 November the Battalion suffered its first fatal casualty in an Eoka ambush. In view of the situation, the morale of the Greek Police was stiffened by the presence of a section of infantry in each of the small police posts in remote rural areas. On the day in question the Officer Commanding D Company set out to visit his posts in a Land Rover driven by Private Baylis, followed by an escort in a 1 ton truck. The posts were on an inland loop road, much of it with sheer cliffs on one side and precipices on the other. The ambush consisted of a bomb hidden in the cliff side and detonated by remote control. Private Baylis, being on the side nearest the explosion, was killed instantly, while Sergeant Cross in the escort vehicle was also wounded. The Company Commander, Major D.A.M. Emms TD, had a narrow escape, but although trapped in a vehicle careering along a narrow mountain road with its driver dead over the wheel he succeeded in bringing it safely to a halt. It was a harsh reminder of the realities of life in Cyprus and came near being repeated a few miles from the same spot a week later. This time however the terrorists miscalculated the distance so that although the vehicle was hit, its occupants escaped injury. On 16 November the reconnaissance and advance parties returned from North Africa. The same day saw the Battalion being partly re-armed by the issue of 260 of the new Belgian Fabrique Nationale (FN) self-loading rifles. They were a replacement for the same number of Number 4 rifles, the reliable but ageing bolt action weapon which had been the standard British individual weapon since the middle of the Second World War.

There followed a couple of local operations, one in Limassol and one in the surrounding countryside, together the inevitable support of Police posts. In one of the latter operations another remote control bomb was detonated by Eoka. Colour-Sergeant Spraggs and Privates Prior and Packman were sufficiently badly wounded in the incident to warrant their being flown out by helicopter. On 13 December the Anti-Tank platoon arrived back with the Battalion, which moved the next day to Nicosia where they joined the rest of 3 Brigade. The Battalion's new role was to form a highly mobile reserve, capable of carrying out large-scale anti-terrorist operations in the whole theatre. They were stationed in Primasole Camp, about three miles out of town on the Troodos road. They spent an undisturbed Christmas, and after it was over said goodbye to the Reservists and retained Regulars who had been held back specifically for the Suez operation, which was by then over.

The New Year opened somewhat inauspiciously when an officer fractured his pelvis and a sergeant broke his back whilst lowering themselves by ropes from a hovering helicopter. This was not altogether good for the morale of the soldiers following them, but fortunately all went well after this initial misfortune.

On 3 January 1957 Major General D.A. Kendrew CBE DSO, the GOC Cyprus District and Director of Operations, paid a visit to the Battalion, followed the next day by an even more exalted personage in Field Marshal Sir John Harding GCB CBE DSO MC, a very distinguished soldier who was then Governor of the island. In the course of his stay with the Battalion he addressed all ranks and visited the Officers' and Sergeants' Messes.

On 15 January, after several preliminary exercises, the Battalion carried out its first operation in Nicosia. This took the form of a search of the Greek quarter and, although no significant finds were reported, valuable lessons were learnt. Two days later it took part in Operation 'Black Mac' to find a gang led by one Afexentiou, second-in-command to Grivas, who were believed to have been flushed from their hiding place on the south coast by the 2nd Battalion The Parachute Regiment which was operating in the area. The whole of 3 Brigade, reinforced by other troops, took part in the operation which lasted a week. The Battalion had no concrete successes to report, but one terrorist was killed and two others captured by other units taking part.

A week later they were out again on Operation 'Brown Jack' which involved another week of hard work which was to be very much the pattern for the future. Guerrilla warfare, by its nature, offers few opportunities for spectacular successes. A few guns here, the occasional suspect there, were all that could reasonably be expected for a great deal of hard work, but the Battalion soon learnt to be philosophical about it.

On 6 February A Company mounted guard on Government House which was an obvious target for terrorist attack, but due to their vigilance nothing untoward occurred.

The Battalion was out again on 18 February for Operation 'Green Dragon', which took place in the wilderness of the Troodos mountains. Here the Battalion re-learnt one of the lessons of Burma, the value of animal transport in difficult country, and used donkeys to carry their wireless sets. They then had three days in camp before going out yet again on Operation 'Lucky Mac'. This operation, which lasted for ten weeks, at least lived up to its name for in the course of it two terrorists (including the notorious Afexentiou) were killed and four captured.

In spite of these and many similar operations the Battalion had a number of solid successes in sport, particularly at cricket and soccer, in which they won the Army Cyprus Championships. By a happy coincidence the 4th/6th Battalion simultaneously won the All-Britain Territorial Army Football while the Depot had a similar success in the Southern Command Minor Units competition.

On 11 April Lieutenant Colonel Tweed, Royal Marines, commanding 40 Commando, very kindly presented the Battalion with a plaque to commemorate the part played by the Anti-Tank platoon in the Suez operations of the previous year.

Operations continued almost ceaselessly, but the Battalion, ever mindful that Internal Security was only one part of their function as soldiers, still found time to initiate the Warrant Officers and Sergeants into the mysteries of drill with the new rifle. It is almost needless to say that, however much they approved of the new rifle for shooting, they much preferred the older weapon for ceremonial use.

In July 1957 came the most shattering blow ever sustained by the Royal Berkshire Regiment in its long history by the announcement that it was to amalgamate with the Wiltshires. It was not of course alone in its shocked reaction for, although the reorganisation was to be implemented in different ways, only a handful of Infantry Regiments were to survive unscathed. It was a far greater blow than that inflicted by the Cardwell Reforms of 1881. Under those earlier reforms the Regiments had changed their titles but their individual Battalions had retained their own identities. It was perhaps ironic that the news should have been received during celebrations to mark the anniversary of Maiwand. There was nothing which could be done about it, for the decision had been taken and it only remained for all concerned to make the proposed new arrangements work. In the meantime there were more pressing matters to be considered.

The most immediately important of these was Exercise 'Kestrel', a large scale amphibious exercise. One way and another it took up most of August and September, after which the Battalion thankfully returned to Nicosia to enjoy a brief period of well earned 'rest', which in all the circumstances it is essential to place in inverted commas.

Christmas festivities lasted from 23–26 December and the Battalion was fortunate that they occurred during a lull in the proceedings. This permitted all ranks to take things easily for a change, although security arrangements were still rigidly enforced, an absolute necessity in the circumstances, since terrorists are always alert to seize unexpected opportunities offered by the slightest signs of relaxation.

On 6 January 1958 the Battalion was informed that it was to move into 50 Independent Infantry Brigade in place of the 3rd Grenadier Guards, the changeover (which did not involve a move) being completed by 14th January. The changeover meant that the role of the Battalion would chiefly be concerned with Internal Security duties in and around Nicosia, which at least offered a change, although there was a widely held opinion that it would be for the worse. Having made the change the Battalion soon had some practical experience in its new role, for on 28 January serious rioting occurred in the Turkish quarter of the city. A composite company, all that was available at the time, was sent out to help a hard pressed company of the Suffolks and eventually got the situation under control by the delivery of a series of brisk baton charges. These charges cooled the ardour of the rioters considerably and doubtless caused some broken heads amongst them. The Battalion also used a combination of fire hoses and pink dyed water as an effective weapon to deter over-ardent women who mobbed the central police station. The women were attempting to obtain the release of their arrested menfolk. RSM L. Hodges nearly had his moustache torn off while attempting to close the heavy police station gates, which were eventually secured after a superhuman struggle. By mid-afternoon the rioting was over, due to a combination of impassioned appeals from various Turkish leaders and a sudden heavy downpour, which damped the ardour of all concerned.

A fortnight later a wandering shepherd in the hills outside the town reported to the Guard Commander at the nearby Makhaeras Monastery that a helicopter had crashed not far away. Part of the guard was at once despatched to the scene but found sadly that both the pilot and his passenger were dead in the wreckage.

About this time two messages were received; the first contained the good news that HRH The Duke of Edinburgh had consented to become Colonel-in-Chief of the new regiment, while the second conveyed the sad information that Captain Peter Chambers MC had been killed in an ambush while serving with the Trucial Oman Scouts. He had been attached to the Regiment from The Royal Hampshires in Eritrea, and his many friends mourned the death of a very gallant officer.

It may be as well to make it clear at this stage that in spite of the operational situation, social life continued to be fairly normal in the circumstances. All the main hotels in Nicosia were open and their restaurants were well patronised by members of the security forces. Although all officers were required to carry pistols off-duty, there appears to have been no occasion when these were required to be used. The main street of the old city, although inevitably dubbed 'Murder Mile' by the more sensational organs of the British Press, was just another shopping area. This was particularly so, perhaps, after the Battalion assumed responsibility for its security. Even at the height of the troubles the Cypriot shopkeepers were invariably courteous to British wives and offered them coffee as a matter of course.

Perhaps the situation may best be summed up by one of the older soldiers in the Battalion who, after perusing one of the more sensational of the British tabloids, was heard to remark that he had never realised what danger he was in until he read it in the papers.

At this time there began a good deal of cross-posting between the Royal Berkshire Regiment and the Wiltshire Regiment. In view of the forthcoming amalgamation this was a very sensible step, although it could have had the effect of lowering morale. Both the more senior officers and their counterparts in the Sergeants Mess had no reason to look forward to the approaching upheaval with anything except apprehension, since it would inevitably mean lack of prospects and redundancies on a large scale. The feeling had existed to some extent in Germany, but there it had been no more than vague doubts about the future, whereas now it was certainties. Nevertheless, morale remained high and people went about their duties cheerfully, which is the sure sign of an efficient and well commanded battalion. The presence of a number of wives also had a steadying influence. Like British service wives the world over they quickly adapted to a new and restrictive routine. If they felt any fears they concealed them bravely, going about their normal business with apparent unconcern.

On 10 April 1958 trouble erupted suddenly in Camp K, the main detention centre, when the Cypriot detainees set fire to their compound. B Company was called in under the overall command of the Battalion Second-in-Command. Order was restored fairly quickly after a series of baton charges

16. The Band and Drums of the 1st Battalion pass the Mayor of Reading during the farewell parade, 14 May 1959.

had brought the shaken inmates to their senses. In the course of the fracas the Company Commander saw someone charging desperately towards him apparently intent on escape. He promptly floored him with a classic straight left, only to find that his victim was an over enthusiastic Turkish photographer, intent on getting some good shots of the proceedings.

On 7 June trouble broke out again, this time in the Turkish sector where some shots were fired, fortunately without effect. B Company had a strenuous few days but soon had things under control. As is usually the way on internal security duties there are always fresh lessons to be learned and the company learnt as it went along. One thing that emerged clearly was the very real fear instilled into the rioters by the mere sight of a few fixed bayonets. They were prepared to face batons and shields with some equanimity but the bayonet was quite a different proposition and they very sensibly fled from the weapon with all the speed they could muster.

C Company was called out to a Greek inspired arson attack on the Turkish Quarter at 2 am one morning. The company found itself having to protect the fire engine, its hoses and the hydrants from further sabotage at the same time as the Turkish firemen were attempting to quench the flames. Even though the water bowser got through, it was not easy in the dark to arrest the Greeks who continued to slash the hoses.

One comment, typical of the British soldier, which was made at the time was that the Battalion's Pakistani 'char wallahs', who followed the troops everywhere should be eligible for the award of the General Service Medal.

Operations were by no means confined to Nicosia, for the Battalion also carried out numerous anti-Eoka operations in the surrounding countryside. C company was even called upon to fight a considerable fire in the tinder-dry forest around the Makheras Monastery about twenty miles from the town. They managed to contain it until help arrived.

This very busy period was followed by a most welcome break, which enabled companies to carry out some training in more orthodox methods of warfare. There were also opportunities for some impromptu range work, and one company at least was fortunate to be near a dam in the mountains in which they swam with great enjoyment.

On 30 September the Battalion was delighted to hear that the Commanding Officer, Lieutenant Colonel Bromhead had been made an Officer of The Order of the British Empire, a further honour to be added to his recent Mention-in-Despatches. He had successfully led the Battalion in various countries and roles for two years and thoroughly deserved it.

On 1 October Brigadier Hogg paid a week's visit to the Battalion where he met many old friends and had a most enjoyable time. During his visit he dined in the Sergeants' Mess where the Warrant Officers and Sergeants wore their new mess kit for the first time. Another change in dress which occurred about this time was the replacement of the old and well-loved China Dragon by the new Wessex Brigade cap badge incorporating the Wyvern. It is probably fair to say that the change was accepted philosophically, but without much enthusiasm.

At this stage the main topic of conversation was the forthcoming amalgamation, and more information on the subject began to filter through. The new title, the date of return to England, the question of colours, certain new items of dress, the future of the Depot and the future location of the new Regimental Headquarters and Museum were amongst the main items which had been agreed. Although much remained to be settled, this information at least provided a basic framework on which to build. The realities of the situation were further brought home by the publication of lists of personnel for premature retirement. By November the list was already formidable and there were ominous promises of more to come.

The time for the return of the Battalion to the United Kingdom was by now fast approaching. On 6 December 1958 the advance party sailed and, after a traditional, although rather subdued Christmas, packing up began. On 25 February 1959 the Battalion, including families, embarked at Limassol and on 7 March they disembarked at Southampton. The National Service members, which comprised the greater part of the Battalion, were naturally interested in leave and a happy quick demobilisation, which they richly deserved after their sterling services. For the Regulars it was not in the main a pleasurable homecoming, especially with the forthcoming amalgamation. At least they could reflect that their efforts of the last two and a half years had not been wasted. In February, just as they were leaving, Archbishop Makarios returned from exile in the Seychelles to become the first president of a new independent republic with a Turkish vice-president to represent the interests of the minority race, transfer of power being completed in December 1959.

Meanwhile the Battalion put a good face on it. After leave and now barely three hundred strong, it re-assembled in Brock Barracks to await the last act of the tragedy, which was not long in coming. There were final visits to the towns which had previously honoured the Regiment with their freedom and then, suddenly, it was all over. On 20 May 1959 the Regimental Colour was trooped in Brock Barracks. The sad event took place in the presence of a large gathering of members and ex-members of the Regiment and was marked, perhaps appropriately, by being a wet and thoroughly gloomy day. Two days later the Colours were laid up in Windsor Castle, where they had been presented in happier circumstances by HM The Queen just three years earlier. In contrast to the ceremonial of their presentation, the laying up was a small, private, forlorn affair, and intensely moving. The Colours were laid up on the Grand Staircase of Windsor Castle. With that final symbolic act over two hundred years of honourable service came to an end for The Royal Berkshire Regiment. However, full discussion and agreement during the period leading up to amalgamation with The Wiltshire Regiment ensured that the traditions of an historic past would continue in the newly formed Duke of Edinburgh's Royal Regiment (Berkshire and Wiltshire).

19. Canon V.J. Pike, Chaplin General to the Queen, officiates before the Colours are taken inside to the apartments.

Previous page:

Top
17. The Colonel of the Regiment with Officers of the 1st Battalion at Brock Barracks, prior to their last guest night, 22 May 1959.

Bottom
18. The Colours are carried into the precincts of Windsor Castle for laying up, 22 May 1959.
Lt Morris (Queen's Colour), 2/Lieut Jones (Regimental Colour), C/Sgt Cross, Sgt Leeder, Sgt Aldridge and RSM Hodges.

The Regimental Depot

On 31 October 1946 No 17 Infantry Training Centre, which had been a joint organisation run in conjunction with the Royal Sussex Regiment, closed down. When this event occurred the former Regimental Depot Party in Brock Barracks reverted to being the Regiment Depot. At the same time No 49 Primary Training Centre also came into existence in the same barracks and, although the two units were technically separate, it was inevitable that they should work in close co-operation.

The barracks had inevitably deteriorated during the war years but, with the help of German Prisoners of War and the whole-hearted co-operation of the Royal Engineers, things soon began to improve. Buildings were refurbished, grass cut, and numerous bulbs planted, so that presently the place began to look its trim, pre-war self.

The Depot was briefly under command of Major G.H.J. Fleming MBE, but Major J.B. Ready soon took over. Its function was to process all Regimental personnel posted from overseas, in hospital, or in staff employment in the United Kingdom. In view of the size of the Regiment at that time, a permanent staff of three officers and fourteen other ranks to carry out these duties was not over-generous, particularly as it was also responsible for administering the Regiment Band,

The Primary Training Centre at first consisted of Headquarters Company, A and B Companies, most of the permanent staff coming either from the other wing of 17 ITC at Colchester and 2nd Infantry Holding Battalion at Aldershot, both these units having been disbanded. It was commanded by Lieutenant Colonel J.C.Q. Harris. Later, in July 1947 the training companies were reduced to just A Company, B Company then being disbanded. Things were difficult at first, due primarily to the constant changes of personnel, but the new unit gradually settled down. Inevitably sports were soon organised, although at first they were mainly confined to hockey and football.

20. The Colonel in Chief visits the Regiment, 1948. HM King George VI accompanied by the Colonel of the Regiment, General Sir Miles Dempsey, with the Commanding Officer, Lieutenant Colonel Harris, and staff of the Regimental Depot on 7 April

On 12 May 1947 HM King George VI graciously consented to become Colonel-in-Chief of the Royal Berkshire Regiment and on 7 April 1948 he visited Brock Barracks, an event described in more detail in Chapter 7.

Soon after the visit the Primary Training Centre was disbanded and all recruit training became the responsibility of the Wessex Group Training Centre at Bulford with each of the six constituent regiments having its own training Company. This meant that Brock Barracks was then occupied by the Regimental Depot only, a small unit consisting of four officers and fourteen other ranks under command of Lieutenant Colonel Harris, who in that year reverted to his substantive rank of Major.

In 1949 the Depot acquired a retired officer for general administrative duties. This was Lieutenant Colonel A.L. Taffs DSO OBE who soon proved a tower of strength to successive commanding officers.

On 25 July 1949 General Sir Miles Dempsey who, in December 1948 had become a Freeman of Reading, re-dedicated the Cenotaph to the memory of the members of the Regiment, to include the 1067 who were killed in action or died on active service in the Second World War. In the course of the ceremony the Colonel of the Regiment placed a copper casket containing a list of their names behind a stone in the Memorial, the stone being engraved 'Casket 1939–1945'. In the same year arrangements were made for the purchase of a site at Wantage on which to build two Memorial cottages for occupation by deserving members of the Regiment. Further cottages were to be built later.

In 1951 arrangements were announced for the resumption of the training of recruits at the Depot, which had, after all, been its principal function for a

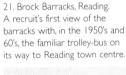

21. Brock Barracks, Reading. A recruit's first view of the barracks with, in the 1950's and 60's, the familiar trolley-bus on its way to Reading town centre.

good many years. The Wessex Brigade Training Centre was to be closed, and after the first six weeks recruits would be sent on to the Wessex Brigade Depot at Exeter to complete their training before posting to battalions. The first Wessex Brigade Colonel, Colonel N.C.E. Kenrick DSO, visited Brock Barracks to discuss arrangements. The majority of the training staff required were to come from the Wessex Brigade Training Centre on closure.

That year too saw a rather belated Honour granted to the Regiment in the form of a Naval Crown, which was in future to be borne on the Regimental Colour. As it had been awarded for services at Copenhagen, almost one hundred and fifty years previously, it could be reasonably classed as delayed.

On 1 December 1951 Major J.T. Cooper assumed command of the Depot vice Major Harris, and after a short break for Christmas immediately became immersed in arrangements for the first intake of recruits which arrived on 17 January 1952. The early squads only served their first six weeks at Brock, but on 16 October the first squad arrived for the whole ten weeks recruits course, after which the regulars among them joined the 1st Battalion. There was, however, no such certainty for the National Service men, who were liable to go to any battalion of the Wessex Brigade. All concerned soon settled down to their new routine, which did much to restore life and activity to the place. All ranks were shocked to hear of the death of King George VI on 6 February 1952, so soon after becoming our Colonel-in-Chief. Next year the Depot contributed a small detachment for the Coronation celebrations in London. The first memorial cottages were also completed and their new occupants moved in. In this year the Regiment was authorised to wear blue lanyards.

On 1 December 1954 Major A.F. Daw took over command of the Depot from Major Cooper. The following year was a busy one with a record number of recruits, two hundred and twenty being under training at the same time. On 3 April 1955 there also occurred the Ceremony of Affiliation of the Berkshire Home Guard to the Royal Berkshire Regiment. Very appropriately the sector commander at the time was Brigadier (Retd) A.P. Aveline CBE MC, who was himself an old and distinguished member of the Regiment.

The first piece of good news in the New Year of 1956 was that General Sir Miles Dempsey had been made a Knight Grand Cross of the British Empire, and that Brigadier Hogg had been elevated to Commander of the same order. Later the Regiment heard with pleasure that he had been selected to succeed General Dempsey as Colonel of the Regiment at the end of the year.

The year also saw the unveiling of two major Second World War memorials. The first, at which Lieutenant Colonel Taffs represented the Regiment on 22 June, was unveiled at Nijmegen to honour those who fell beyond the Seine and had no known graves; the second was similarly intended to honour those who fell in Sicily and Italy. It was situated at the War Cemetery at Cassino and the Regiment was represented by Major (Retd) R. D.C. West who had served in the theatre with the 10th Battalion. About this time it was announced that the Battle Honours Committee had finished its long and arduous task and would shortly issue its report. In the event it appeared early in 1957, those of the Royal Berkshire Regiment being finally published in Army Order 86 of

22. Major Myatt taking the Salute at parade of National Servicemen, 1958.

1957 on 31 July 1957. The list was a long and honourable one, although it is ironic that we may anticipate events, slightly, and comment that its publication almost coincided with the one announcing amalgamation.

Brigadier Hogg took over as Colonel of the Regiment on 22 November 1956, and on 7 January 1957 Major F. Myatt MC succeeded Major Daw in command of the Regimental Depot. Although they did not know it at the time they were both destined (like the Commanding Officer of the 1st Battalion) to have the sad distinction of being the last officers ever to hold their respective posts, a fact finally revealed to them in July.

Meanwhile life went on as usual, although inevitably the approaching amalgamation gave rise to a host of additional problems, for many of which there were no precedents. Training of course continued at full swing, as did sport in which the Depot won the Southern Command Minor Units Soccer. Other activities included a successful Civil Defence Day, the Old Comrades Association weekend and the usual parades and ceremonies for Tofrek and Maiwand. On 27 June the Dunkirk Memorial was unveiled by the Queen Mother, the Regiment being represented by Lieutenant Colonel Harris.

By 1958 a steady stream of old friends had begun to depart for civil life. Reasonable compensation terms, the famous Golden Bowlers, were available, and as industry was then buoyant the bulk of the departures were able to get good jobs which at least softened the blow.

On 30 April Major General B.A. Coad CB CBE DSO, Colonel of the Wiltshire Regiment and Colonel-elect of the new amalgamated regiment, took the salute at a passing out parade. It was almost the last one to be held, for the final batch of recruits left on 13 August that year. Their departure coincided with an increase in Territorial recruiting, so the Depot was able to give some welcome, if temporary, assistance in training pending the departure of almost the entire training staff to other postings or civil life.

Two more memorials to the Second World War were unveiled in 1958, one in Rangoon, at which it was not possible for the Regiment to be represented, and a second at Brookwood in memory of all those who had been lost at sea, in commando raids, or had otherwise died in circumstances which made it impossible to mark their graves. It was opened by HM The Queen, the Regiment being represented by the Officer Commanding the Depot. At this stage all the efforts of the remaining Depot staff were concentrated on the forthcoming amalgamation.

The two Colonels met regularly, as did the Regimental Committee, and although there were occasionally grave differences between them, it was always possible to reach a compromise in the end. Once the broad decisions had been reached the task of implementing them inevitably fell to the two Depot Commanders. Fortunately they got on well together. Time was short and there was no precedent for much which had to be done, with the result that sometimes even major decisions were made over working lunches. It is however probably fair to say that almost all of them have stood the test of time. Many of the problems were concerned with the disposal of large quantities of Regimental property for which no use could be found in the new Regiment. Bearing in mind the fact that six regular Battalions, first, second and third Militia of both regiments, plus two regimental depots had to be reduced to a single unit it will be appreciated that the problems were huge. The surplus silver inevitably attracted London dealers, who buzzed round like so many bluebottles. However, they were all held successfully at bay, all unwanted items being sold within the Regiment. Great quantities of lesser stuff of little sale value were simply burnt, and a fire on some wasteland near the Pioneers shop burned for days.

In the middle of these sad scenes, unprecedented in the history of the Regiment, the Depot suffered a grievous loss in the death of Lieutenant Colonel (Retd) Taffs, the Administrative Officer. He had for some time been in bad health, and the prospect of amalgamation held no joys for him, but he nevertheless did all he could to make it work. He literally died in harness, and everyone was deeply saddened.

Very fortunately a recently retired officer of the Wiltshires, Lieutenant Colonel L.H. Wood OBE, volunteered to fill the gap at short notice and, although completely new to the job, he soon had everything under complete control, to the relief of the Depot Commander who at that particular period was a very busy man.

Early in 1959 the Battalion, at that stage little more than three hundred strong, returned to England and after leave were mainly accommodated in the Depot, with others at Ranikhet Camp Tilehurst. They occupied some of the 1886 vintage married quarters which, although derelict for many years, were soon made habitable by the very considerable efforts of the Garrison Engineer. The Depot returned to life for a few short weeks while the Battalion said goodbye to the county of Berkshire; the Colours were finally trooped on 20 May, and two days later they were laid up in Windsor Castle. With their going the Royal Berkshire Regiment ceased to exist as a regular unit.

7 The 4th/6th Battalion (TA)

After what may be called a sabbatical year the Territorial Army was reformed in the summer of 1947. So far as the Regiment was concerned there was little to build on, for the 5th and 7th Battalions (both originally raised in London) had already faded away, their residual welfare funds later forming a welcome contribution to the OCA Benevolent Fund. Apart from the original 4th Battalion, the only other Territorial unit to have been raised in Berkshire was the 6th Battalion, and the new unit was therefore given the title The 4th/6th Battalion The Royal Berkshire Regiment, although it continued to carry the pre-war Colours of the 4th. This was a sensible move since it not only helped to recruit old hands from both county battalions, but also perpetuated the title of an excellent unit.

Since the formation of the TA in 1907 general administration had been in the hands of County Associations. This was still the case and it was on the advice of the local association that the War Office Selection Board appointed Lieutenant Colonel H.P. Verey TD to command the newly formed 4th/6th Battalion. A prominent and long established resident of the county with over twenty years Territorial service he was, in every respect, the right man at the right time. He was ably assisted as second in command by Major P.H.A. Brownrigg DSO, one of the Regiment's most distinguished war time Territorials, who later took over command. Inevitably, after five years of war, the country was surfeited with military service and recruiting slowed to a trickle at about the hundred mark although most of these were good war time material including some capable Company commanders. In retrospect shortage of numbers was no great handicap. The role of the TA at this time was to hold and train, on a part time basis, National Service men who had completed their two years Colour service. Until this system became established in a year or two a pause to enable NCOs to be trained and a firm administrative base established was time well spent. To this end annual camps were revived, the first with an unmistakable pre-war flavour at Chickerell near Weymouth. Regular assistance was on a generous scale to compensate for the loss of the training teams which the home regular Battalion had provided in those leisurely days before the war. In addition to the Adjutant, Quartermaster and Regimental Sergeant Major, there was a full time Training Major and twelve Permanent Staff Instructors.

In April 1948 HM King George VI, Colonel in Chief of the Regiment, visited the Depot and, after lunching, went on to the Forbury Gardens escorted by General Sir Miles Dempsey and the Officer Commanding the Depot. Here a Guard of Honour of three officers and 50 men with the band of the Royal Marines, Portsmouth, was drawn up. His Majesty was met by the Mayor before mounting a small dais in front of the Maiwand Lion for the Royal Salute. There were many old comrades present including some officers with service going back to Tofrek.

At this time too, Colonel O. Pearce-Serocold CMG VD retired from being Honorary Colonel of the 4th/6th Battalion. He had first joined the Berkshire Volunteers in 1885 and had commanded the 4th Royal Berkshires for the first eleven years of their life, finally handing over command in 1916 after a year's active service in France. He was succeeded by Colonel G.S. Field OBE TD who had also served with the Battalion in the Great War and had commanded it in the early thirties. He in turn was followed by Brigadier K.P. Smith OBE an ex-regular officer of the Regiment and a colourful and endearing personality. Commissioned in 1916 he had commanded the 6th Battalion in Northern Ireland in the early years of the war. In 1959, with the amalgamation of the Royal Berkshire and Wiltshire Regiments, Brigadier Hogg who until then had been Colonel of the Regiment, became Honorary Colonel of the 4th/6th Battalion, followed in due course by Lieutenant Colonel Verey the last of the line. It was to be this officer's last sad duty to hand over the 4th/6th Battalion's Colours to the Bishop of Reading for laying up.

In 1951 there were signs that the era of small numbers and fairly leisurely camps was drawing to a close. In this year National Service men began to appear, with muted enthusiasm, for their compulsory training. The following year the international scene had worsened, the temperature had dropped and the Berlin Wall was shortly to rise amid the ruins of the city. 'Z' Reservists swamped the Battalion in camp at Windmill Hill on Salisbury Plain, where sadly a shell from a supporting battery burst among them, killing one and gravely wounding another. The Battalion was in no way to blame and everyone understood that in serious training such things could happen. It was remarked that, after the incident, the Company involved marched past the CO with the rhythm and steadiness of first class regular troops.

1953 saw the coronation of HM Queen Elizabeth II and a detachment with Colours under command of Major D.A.H. Hartley-Russell formed part of the marching column. Earlier in the year Lieutenant Colonel Hayward had taken over command. A regular Royal Berkshireman, well experienced in command, he had a style which, though often irreverent, was all his own and was well suited to his reluctant but good natured soldiers – if not to Divisional Commanders. He was greatly helped by an outstandingly good body of National Service subalterns. There were still some competent company commanders, but the war was seven years gone and the next one might be closer. Camp this year was at Stanford PTA where by good luck the 1st Battalion was in residence thus giving rise to much hospitality and even a cricket match. There was also a stupendous quantity of ammunition of all natures which the Battalion was encouraged to fire off, apparently to impress a visiting American Colonel and his Dutch colleague from NATO. The following year at Penhale, on the Cornish coast, things seemed more civilised. So that troops could see them and pay compliments the Colours were uncased daily and lodged outside the Guardroom. 129 Brigade Headquarters were just down the road and it is worth remarking that the DAA & QMG had held the same appointment in the same Brigade in Normandy as also had the GSO3 (1). The GSO (3) Ops had been a GSO2 and the Staff Captain had been a BRASCO. The 4th/6th Battalion should have been in good hands.

Nuclear war began to be discussed at this time and fallout became a subject for the annual indoor exercise in January. Back at Windmill Hill in 1955 the Sappers, resourceful as ever, made commendable imitations of atomic bombs out of forty gallon drums stuffed with assorted combustibles. This was part of an exercise named after an ancient Saxon conflict which the troops, with justification, called 'Effing Down'. The camp itself was a standing tented habitation occupied without interval by a succession of TA Brigades. When the 4th/6th Battalion arrived the grass in the tents had been worn by the pressure of many bodies into small chalk pits in which the troops were invited to strive for such rest as the training programme allowed them, which was little enough. The cook house too showed signs of eccentricity, but through it all the Battalion showed commendable, if sardonic, patience, a tribute to Colonel Hayward's personal touch.

The following year, under command of Lieutenant Colonel J.L.R. Metcalf, an ex-regular, the 4th/6th Battalion was in the old fort at Tregantle in Cornwall training for its new role as part of the NATO Reserve. This entailed mobilising two TA Divisions and getting them onto the west bank of the Rhine in time to support BAOR, as it recoiled before the Fantasian avalanche. To this end exercises for divisional and brigade headquarters, generically known as Javelin, were held on the continent. It was in this year that National Service men began to fade out to the sorrow of all who were left. They were good men and it was an honour to command them. Their presence had also given a sense of purpose and national unity.

It was also the year when the 4th/6th Battalion put into practice certain lessons remembered from the past. Chief among these was that wireless sets left long in store cannot be assumed to work first time they are taken out of store, especially in the hands of less than fully trained signallers. In the same way, vehicles drawn from a Vehicle Reserve Depot did not possess the same characteristics as fully maintained ones and consequently march tables were apt to go awry. The Battalion therefore always had a 'Jack up' parade before an exercise, when drivers and operators were wedded to their equipment which was then forced to function in the simplest conditions. It did not matter who was on the set or at the wheel provided it worked because, if it did not, the exercise was guaranteed to be a disaster. Similarly much time was spent reconnoitring training areas to make sure that what the map implied was really true. By these and other means a reputation was established for tactical efficiency. Likewise a reputation for administrative efficiency was acquired by the simplest expedient of officers dining at stated times, properly dressed, thus giving an excellent mess staff a chance to give of its best. All this was not achieved without generating some envy among neighbouring units who could not understand why it was right to dress for dinner but equally right to walk to Church in shirt sleeves and stable belts.

Behind the scenes things did not always go smoothly. There was an anxious time when the TA Association wanted two battalions to share a mess. It took long and forceful argument to convince them, reluctantly, that this would be contrary to one of the principal reasons for going to camp. There was an even

23. 4th/6th Battalion Football
Team 1957.

Back row:
CSM G. Bishop, Pte B. Chapman, Pte B. Buckle, L/Cpl B. Wheeler, Pte P. Passsey, Pte D. Harding,
Sgt E. Jones, RSM L. R. Hodges

Centre row:
Pte I. Borton, Pte T. Lambert, Lieut Col J. L. R. Metcalf (Commanding Officer), Pte B. Guttridge (Captain),
Capt G. P. Savill (Adjutant), Pte J. Low, Pte R. Cooper

Inset:
Cpl R. Mortimer, Pte M. Werrell

more alarming ordeal when they tried to evict the 4th/6th Battalion from its ancestral home in Brock Barracks, a move only frustrated by a flanking operation initiated by a sympathetic Brigadier. On yet another occasion some Royal Berkshire soldiers were discovered erecting the officers mess tent for the 5th Gloucesters who chanced to have an ex-Commanding Officer working in Records. The Colonel of the Regiment was visiting the Battalion at the time and supported the Commanding Officer in his protest to the same Brigadier. The contest was lost, but with honour.

In 1957 the RSM, Mr Hodges, reported that he had discovered among the remaining National Service men the entire football team of the 1st Battalion. He invited them to join him in an empty hut from which they all emerged as volunteers, subsequently winning the TA Football cup on three occasions. Since they were all trained soldiers it was only natural that a certain amount of PT should begin to appear in training programmes. The 4th/6th Battalion also won the Southern Command Cross Country Championship, but without the help of its footballers. As the National Service element diminished and the passing years reduced the proportion of war time volunteers, the numbers game intruded increasingly into the scheme of things. Berkshire was not a good recruiting area. Employment was relatively high and potential officers tended to be attracted towards the upmarket regiments of the City of London. The problem might have been countered by over-emphasising the appeal of the clubs, which existed wherever companies were located, and by lowering standards. However, the 4th/6th Battalion preferred to take the line that the men they wanted would join what they thought was a good unit and to weed out, as mercifully as possible, those who did not measure up to the serious business in hand. In consequence, although it was not the strongest battalion in the TA, it was for many years regarded as one of the best. This opinion is one with which those who had the honour and good fortune to serve in it were inclined to agree. Numbers apart, there was always at all levels a nucleus of first class material whose presence made all the effort worthwhile.

There was also a strong element of former regular soldiers in the 4th/6th Battalion which helped to cement a close liaison between the Regimental Depot and the 1st Battalion. They ranged from that essential technician, the sanitary corporal, to the Second in Command Major Cooper, whose last regular Regimental appointment had been as CO of the Depot. There was also Major Paxton, one of whose claims to fame was his impersonation of a Sandhurst Staff Sergeant. The Sergeants' Mess also had its quota including representatives from the Household Cavalry and the Royal Fusiliers as well as Drum Major Jones and Sergeant Allen, both 'of ours'. The latter had been Mess Corporal before the war and more recently Mess Sergeant of the First Battalion. His polished ministrations maintained standards which never failed to create favourable impressions on visiting senior officers.

September 1958 saw the arrival of Lieutenant Colonel L.J.L. Hill MC to assume command, a regular officer from the 1st Battalion in Cyprus of great experience and energy. His appointment however did not imply any dearth of local talent. Rather, the imminent amalgamation of The Royal Berkshire and Wiltshire Regiments, and the consequent closing of the Regimental Depot at Brock Barracks, made the presence in Reading of a professional soldier of more than ordinary ability essential.

The onus of becoming the sole remaining unit of the Regiment after amalgamation in June 1959 was accepted with vigour by all ranks and it was fitting that RSM Price of the Wiltshire Regiment should be posted in as if to emphasise a new era as part of the Duke of Edinburgh's Royal Regiment.

1959 thus saw the major ceremonial occasions both of the amalgamation and, closer to home, the great centenary celebrations of the formation of the Berkshire Rifle Volunteers in 1859. Sixteen officers and 140 other ranks paraded in the Forbury Gardens at Reading before a distinguished audience which uniquely included no less than seven Mayors of Berkshire towns. The Chairman of the TA Association, Air Marshal Sir Robert Saundby, took the salute when, with Colours flying, band playing and bayonets fixed the 4th/6th Battalion did justice to RSM Price's meticulous preparations and gave rise to the rumour 'they are really regulars'. The Maiwand Lion, in honour of an earlier generation of Berkshire soldiers, gazed down approvingly, while the deluge which swamped the scene only served to emphasise that the Volunteers continued to be ready to play their part in the defence of the realm whatever the conditions. A loyal message was sent to, and a gracious reply received from, Her Majesty.

The centenary dinner held in the Great Western Hotel was attended by some 120 officers and guests including Captain C.L. Lloyd MC of Lockinge who presented the important and notable portrait of his ancestor Lord Wantage VC, the first Commanding Officer of the Volunteers in Berkshire.

On Sunday 11 October the Church Parade in St Mary's Butts, Reading, was taken by the Bishop of Reading with the lesson being read by Air Marshal Saundby. The Mayor and council of Reading and many distinguished guests attended this conclusion to the celebrations.

It is interesting to recall that the original formation of the Volunteers, so fittingly observed, was part of a spontaneous, nation-wide and privately financed response to the launch of an armoured, screw driven French warship, the first of its kind in the world. This vessel, *La Gloire*, was capable of crossing the channel overnight in any weather. Britain had no counter to it and it appeared to threaten the defeat of the Royal Navy and the invasion of the United Kingdom. In those uncomplicated days it needed only such a perceived threat to bring the men of Great Britain to arms and at their own expense.

1959–1961 were golden years for the 4th/6th Battalion in training, ceremonial and sport. The confidential report for 1961 classified it as 'one of the best TA units in the country' and the chairman paid a special tribute to all ranks in his annual address to the Association.

The 4th/6th Battalion's achievements and successes crossed almost the whole spectrum of its activities. Two further years as winners of the TA Football Cup: for the first time winners of the 43rd (Wessex) Division unit shooting championship, now shot with the new rifles and machine guns; winners of the Divisional cross country championship and runners-up in the Duke of Edinburgh's Trophy Competition. The Band and Drums continued to give very high levels of performance and the Intelligence section, which included a solicitor and three articled clerks, became outstanding assets in Brigade exercises.

One unusual honour which fell to the 4th/6th Battalion in this period was the laying up of two sets of old Colours which had until then been kept in Brock Barracks. On two consecutive days in July 1960 those of the 3rd (Militia) Battalion, which had for long adorned the Officers' Mess, were installed in the Town Hall at Abingdon, and those borne by the 1st Battalion in the period 1908–1956 were placed in Saint Michael's Church, Wallingford. It was fitting that this should have been done by the last surviving unit of the Royal Berkshire Regiment.

Training in Civil Defence and in nuclear war settings both at annual camps and at weekend exercises took the 4th/6th Battalion not only to the Lake District, Snowdonia and the New Forest, but to the beaches of Normandy.

'Exercise Autumn Crocus' in October was a specially unique Battalion week-end exercise for the TA. Organised by the battalion with the help of Southern Command and 43 Wessex Division HQ, it provided post war volunteer service with valuable experience at unit level. Interservice cooperation and a sea voyage across the channel with *HMS Loch Fyne* and *Finisterre* 'landing' on the D Day beaches close to Cherbourg to meet the 'enemy' provided by the French 21st Chasseurs à Pieds Regiment. The Battalion embarked on Friday night returning to Brock Barracks on Sunday evening via Poole and Portsmouth. The volunteers resumed their civilian careers on Monday. The exercise gave Territorial recruiting a major boost which, with military exhibitions throughout the county, took the Battalion strength to forty per cent of establishment.

At Wallingford the MP for Abingdon, Airey Neave, later to be brutally and stupidly assassinated by the IRA, and Colonel the Honourable Gordon Palmer, who had commanded the Berkshire Yeomanry and was to become Lord Lieutenant for the county, both spoke at a public meeting in the Town Hall.

A major success during these years of Government retrenchment was yet another victory in the defence of Brock Barracks as the 4th/6th Battalion's training centre. The Director of Quartering himself held a meeting at the Barracks to hear views of powerful conflicting interests and finally removed uncertainty to the benefit of the units continuity.

In April 1961 Lieutenant Colonel R.A. Plackett TD succeeded to the command. A pre-war Territorial from the Essex Regiment he had served in the fighting in North Africa and Italy mainly with the 4th Indian Division. Experienced and competent, he had been recommended for command for several years but circumstances had decreed a preponderance of regular or neo-regular commanding officers. Not-withstanding this potential disappointment both he and his successor had soldiered on loyally and cheerfully, as befitted good Territorial officers. Under him the cycle of activity continued, though unseen, official hands would soon be rocking the boat. The 4th/6th Battalion found itself in 128 Brigade and there was a change in War Establishment involving the farming out of support weapons among rifle companies with consequent problems in training scattered support platoons. Emphasis was still on conventional infantry training though Civil Defence began to assume increased importance. Standards remained high, particularly in weapon training, and in 1962 HRH The Duke of Edinburgh visited Brock Barracks to present his trophy to Lieutenant Colonel Plackett and his victorious team who had won it for the first time. Annual camps were at Penhale and Stanford PTA, with everyone in their usual good spirits. Officers and NCOs were of notably good quality but recruiting remained a nagging anxiety. In 1963, under command of Lieutenant Colonel C.H. Willing TD, a Sandhurst trained war time officer with twenty years service, the Rifle meeting was combined with a recruiting drive. Coaches to the ranges, free meals, drinks and free shooting were offered to the youth of Berkshire who appeared in gratifying numbers. Subsequent analysis revealed that at least one recruit could be attributed to this expensive effort.

At this time too the number of days pay which volunteers could draw was reduced, thus seriously restricting the scope for ambitious and interesting exercises. All ranks turned to individual and sub-unit training and to administration of the Football team, still in the forefront of local and TA competitions and about to defeat the winners of the Regular Army Cup by four goals to nil. Now the Regimental Magazine of the day makes the first light hearted reference to 'Ever Readies'. But a more sombre note is soon struck and articles became longer and more thoughtful, doing credit to their anonymous authors. There is a camp at Devizes with fire-fighting as the main subject, as though no one quite knew what use to make of the TA. Then it seems there was a move afoot to raise a Volunteer Reserve Battalion for the Wessex Brigade, as it then was, and mention is made of lists of men volunteering for different states of readiness. Every effort was obviously made to keep people informed and in 1965 it emerged that there would in future be one Territorial and Volunteer Reserve in three tiers. The first would be the old Supplementary Reserve of Docks Operating Companies and the like; the second a fully equipped and up to strength reserve Battalion, the Wessex Volunteers (TAVR), with Headquarters at Exeter and one company in Reading; and thirdly an equally widespread but less well prepared Territorial and Army Volunteer Reserve III (Territorials).

In 1966 Lieutenant Colonel J.A. Sellers MBE, a regular officer, took over command of the now sadly moribund 4th/6th Battalion. Since he was also Commanding Officer designate of the Wessex Volunteers his task was to raise the new Battalion from all the TA Units in the south west, and since they were all under strength this had to be regardless of arm or service and with an appropriate proportion of officers and NCOs. This occasioned much travelling, conferring, heart searching and some hurt feelings. All the time he was conscious of the need to keep the life of his own Battalion going till the end.

The end was not far off now. The active service record had been distinguished; a Company of Volunteers had gone to the Boer War; two Battalions of Territorials had gone to the Great War; the 4th, 5th and 6th Battalions had gone to Hitler's War, and between them they had amassed nearly thirty Battle Honours. On 18 March 1967 two guards with the Colours, Band and Drums paraded in the Forbury Gardens supported by a gathering of Old Comrades. Dignitaries of the County and the Borough took the salute. The parade marched off to form at the entrance to Saint Laurence's Church and to present arms as the Colours, presented by King Edward VII in 1909, were marched off for the last time. So it was all over and the last surviving unit of The Royal Berkshire Regiment had passed into history.

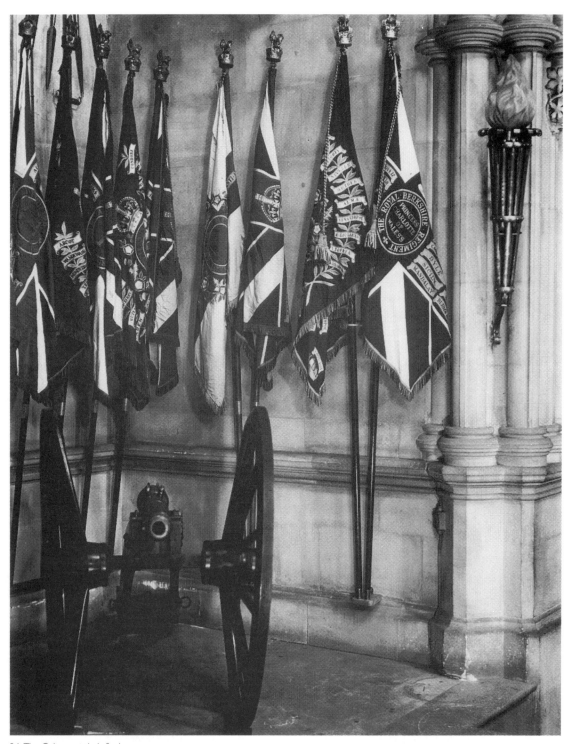

24. The Colours at their final
resting place on the Grand
Staircase of Windsor Castle
alongside those of the disbanded
Irish regiments.

Index